Cambridge Elements

Elements in Metaphysic
edited by
Tuomas E. Tahko
University of Bristol

METAONTOLOGY

Kris McDaniel
University of Notre Dame

Shaftesbury Road, Cambridge CB2 8EA, United Kingdom

One Liberty Plaza, 20th Floor, New York, NY 10006, USA

477 Williamstown Road, Port Melbourne, VIC 3207, Australia

314–321, 3rd Floor, Plot 3, Splendor Forum, Jasola District Centre, New Delhi – 110025, India

103 Penang Road, #05-06/07, Visioncrest Commercial, Singapore 238467

Cambridge University Press is part of Cambridge University Press & Assessment, a department of the University of Cambridge.

We share the University's mission to contribute to society through the pursuit of education, learning and research at the highest international levels of excellence.

www.cambridge.org
Information on this title: www.cambridge.org/9781009618502

DOI: 10.1017/9781009119870

© Kris McDaniel 2025

This publication is in copyright. Subject to statutory exception and to the provisions of relevant collective licensing agreements, no reproduction of any part may take place without the written permission of Cambridge University Press & Assessment.

When citing this work, please include a reference to the DOI 10.1017/9781009119870

First published 2025

A catalogue record for this publication is available from the British Library

ISBN 978-1-009-61850-2 Hardback
ISBN 978-1-009-11344-1 Paperback
ISSN 2633-9862 (online)
ISSN 2633-9854 (print)

Cambridge University Press & Assessment has no responsibility for the persistence or accuracy of URLs for external or third-party internet websites referred to in this publication and does not guarantee that any content on such websites is, or will remain, accurate or appropriate.

For EU product safety concerns, contact us at Calle de José Abascal, 56, 1°, 28003 Madrid, Spain, or email eugpsr@cambridge.org

Metaontology

Elements in Metaphysics

DOI: 10.1017/9781009119870
First published online: June 2025

Kris McDaniel
University of Notre Dame
Author for correspondence: Kris McDaniel, kmcdani1@nd.edu

Abstract: Metaontology is the branch of philosophy that focuses on questions that naturally arise when doing ontology. This Element offers the reader (some of) the elements of metaontology by way of an opinionated overview of (some of) its central arguments and positions. The first section of this element focuses on whether there are nonexistent objects. It discusses historical figures such as Suarez, Brentano, Twardowski, and Meinong, as well as contemporary figures such as Lewis, van Inwagen, Thomasson, and Zalta. The second section focuses on whether ontological questions are trivial to answer and whether ontological debates are merely verbal debates. Can there be different concepts of existence or different meanings of "exists" or other ontological expressions? If ontological questions are nontrivial, are they nontrivial only if a substantive metaphysical view is true? Even if there aren't different senses of "exist," might there be different modes of being or ways to exist?

Keywords: metaontology, deflationalism, easy ontology, nonexistence, ontological pluralism

© Kris McDaniel 2025

ISBNs: 9781009618502 (HB), 9781009113441 (PB), 9781009119870 (OC)
ISSNs: 2633-9862 (online), 2633-9854 (print)

Contents

Introduction   1

1 Are There Nonexistent Objects?   4

2 Are Ontological Debates Nonsubstantive?   30

Summary Remarks   61

References   62

Introduction

As one would expect from its title, this Element offers you (some of) the elements of metaontology by way of an opinionated overview of (some of) the central arguments and positions. It is opinionated in three ways. I evaluate ideas and arguments as I present them, rather than present them with an air of neutrality. The selection of ideas and arguments to discuss here was not mandatory: though I have a limited word count, there are other metaontological topics that could have been discussed instead. Finally, my conception of metaontology is capacious, which is why it's clear to me that other topics could have been selected. This conception will be presented (rather than argued for) in the remainder of this section.

Metaontology is the branch of philosophy that focuses on questions that naturally arise in the context of doing ontology. Although the idea of metaontology itself might initially strike one as a bit too meta, the development of metaontology as a discipline is both unsurprising and welcome. Every human activity generates philosophical questions, including doing ontology. Should philosophers ignore those philosophical questions simply because they are questions about philosophy? Of course not!

For now, let us provisionally characterize ontological inquiry as inquiry into what there is and what exists. Whether this provisional characterization should ultimately be a definitional characterization is itself a metaontological question, and it is a question that is closely related to other metaontological questions, such as the question of which concept of ontology is most fruitful to adopt, and the even more meta question of whether we can decide this question of fruitfulness independently of deciding the first-order question of what there is and what exists. But perhaps discussing this is jumping headfirst into the weeds before we've looked at the rest of the garden. So, let's take a step back.

One way to demarcate various questions, topics, and themes in metaontology is by appealing to standard (but not sacred) ways of demarcating the main subfields of philosophy, and discussing how those subfields overlap with metaontology. That's what I'll do here.[1]

Epistemology focuses on questions about knowing, evidence, and reasons for belief. One branch of metaontology focuses on epistemological questions about ontology. Can ontological beliefs be justified? Do we have ontological knowledge? Philosophy is a dodgy business – so you might think that it's unlikely that we have any. But we do have some ontological knowledge, albeit negative or

---

[1] See also McDaniel (2020: chapter 6), which characterizes metaontology in a similar way and covers some metaontological questions (such as the question about the value of metaphysics) not discussed here.

conditional knowledge. For example, we know that if there are any numbers, there are all the numbers, rather than all of them except the number 17, and we know that whatever the correct answer is to the question of when some objects compose a whole, it's not that these objects are all in New Jersey. Maybe thinking through how we can know these things will shed light on what other things in ontology can be known.[2]

The philosophy of language focuses on questions about meaning, reference, objectivity, and truth. One branch of metaontology focuses on such questions about characteristically ontological vocabulary. What do we mean by "exists," "there is," or "some"?[3] Do ontological expressions really have the function they seem to have, namely, to aid in describing reality, or do they have a covert purpose?[4] Given roughly how we use these terms, were other meaning for them possible, or does our rough use of these terms suffice to secure the meanings that they have, perhaps because they are the only available meanings to be had? Or are there equally good things that could be meant by these expressions?

Ethics focuses on questions about value, right and wrong, justice and fairness, virtue and vice. A third branch of metaontology focuses on ethical questions about ontological theorizing. Here are some of them. To what extent should our ethical theorizing constrain our ontological theorizing? Can considerations of what is just or good be relevant to which ontological theories we should endorse? If a true ontological theory has implications that we take to be unfair or unjust, is there something we can do to make that theory no longer be true?[5] Can there be a conceptual ethics that would evaluate not what we should do but rather what concepts we should have?[6] Are key ontological concepts or terms evaluative concepts or terms, and if so, which ones?[7]

Metaphysics focuses on those questions about reality that are not settled by empirical investigations. A fourth branch of metaontology focuses on metaphysical questions about ontology itself. Does ontology itself have metaphysical

---

[2] This idea is pursued further in McDaniel (2020: 215–227).
[3] There seem to be eight answers to the question of which of these expressions are synonymous. (The eighth is that they are all meaningless expressions.) Roughly, van Inwagen (1998) takes them to be all synonymous, while a standard way of being a Meinongian is to lump "there is" and "some" together and distinguish them from "exists," but on Priest's (2005: 13–14) version of Meinongianism, "there is" and "exists" are lumped together and distinguished from "some."
[4] A standard conception of ontology is one in which ontological claims are descriptive claims that aim to describe reality, but Flocke (2021) defends an *expressivist* account of ontological claims according to which they express noncognitive mental states such as the acceptance of norms. In a similar vein, McDaniel (2017b: 180–181) develops (but does not defend) a noncognitivist account of metaphysical fundamentality.
[5] This idea is discussed in Jenkins (2020).
[6] See the papers in Burgess, Cappelen, and Plunkett (2021) for different putative answers to this question.
[7] See again Flocke (2021) and McDaniel (2017b).

presuppositions?[8] If so, what are they, and if they are no longer presupposed, is a kind of inquiry similar to ontological inquiry still possible – and if so, what would this kind of inquiry be? What is the nature of being or existence? Does it make sense to even ask if being or existence has a nature?

Just as there is no clean separation between ontology and metaontology, there is no clean separation between the history of ontology and the history of metaontology. Questions about the metaontological views of our deceased predecessors, as well as questions about their arguments for them, belong to the history of metaontology, but insofar as we pursue answers to these questions because we think of a particular historical figure or tradition that their views were correct or their arguments sound, they belong to metaontology as well. The first section discusses a few figures from the history of metaontology.

Metaontology is a wide-ranging and vibrant field of philosophy. No book this size could do it justice. Accordingly, I won't try to represent the full glory of metaontology here. The remainder of this introduction is a preview of the remainder of the Element.

I provisionally characterized ontological inquiry as inquiry into what there is and what exists. This provisional understanding immediately raises the questions of whether what there is and what exists coincide, and if so, whether they coincide as a matter of necessity, and if so, why they coincide as a matter of necessity. In short, are there nonexistent objects, and if not, why are there no such things?

The question of whether there are nonexistent objects is the focus of Section 1. This section discusses some of the main historical positions on the status of allegedly nonexistent objects called "beings of reason," and discusses historical figures such as Suarez, Brentano, Twardowski, and Meinong. It also discusses some of the main arguments against nonexistent objects in the contemporary literature, with a special focus on arguments from philosophers such as Thomasson, van Inwagen, Lewis, and Zalta. Two sorts of arguments will be discussed, which are roughly (1) arguments that there are no such things at all as the putative nonexistents and (2) arguments that there are such things as (some of) the putative nonexistents, but these putative nonexistents do in fact exist.

Section 2 will focus on whether ontological questions are trivial to answer and whether ontological debates are merely verbal debates. Can there can be different concepts of existence or different meanings of "exists" or other ontological expressions? Do we even need to theorize about objects in terms of existence? If ontological questions are nontrivial, what if anything explains why they are nontrivial? Are they nontrivial only if a substantive ontological or

---

[8] See McDaniel (2020: 235–242) for a discussion of this question.

metaphysical view is true? And even if there aren't different senses of "exist," might there be different modes of being or ways to exist?

These questions are important questions, and central to much current metaontological discussion. The richness of the field means difficult decisions about what to cover – but I hope the ensuing discussion whets your appetite for more metaontology.

1 Are There Nonexistent Objects?

1.1 The Problem of Nonexistents

Are there things that do not exist? At first, this question seems easy to answer: of course not. How could something be without existing? Aren't the ideas of being something and being an existing thing the same? On the other hand, it seems that we can produce examples of things that don't exist. Santa Claus doesn't exist, thankfully, but sadly neither does Spider-Man. But Santa Claus and Spider-Man are not identical, and though they have some features in common, they also differ: although both typically wear costumes with a lot of red, Santa Claus does a deeper dive into the private information of people than social media companies, while Spider-Man knows that with great power, there must also come great responsibility. So, there are at least two things – Santa Claus and Spider-Man – that do not exist. These two examples seemingly form the tip of a large nonexistent iceberg containing innumerable creatures of myth and fable. For example, no Greek God exists, and neither do any of the Roman Gods, but aren't the Roman Gods the same Gods just with different names? No Norse Gods exist either, but the Norse Gods are not the same nonexistent Gods as the Greek Gods.

The case that I've stated for nonexistent objects seems reasonably straightforward: We can distinguish nonexistent objects from one another, which means that we can count nonexistent objects; we can count nonexistent objects only if there are nonexistent objects; therefore, there are nonexistent objects. In short, nonexistent objects are available to be quantified over. Among contemporary philosophers, the view that there are nonexistent objects is called "Meinongianism," named after Alexius Meinong, about whom more will be said later in this section.

There is a second, related argument that stems from answering affirmatively a fundamental question that will be raised again and again through the history of philosophy: does "thinking of" denote a two-place relation between a thinker and what that thinker is thinking of? If "thinking of" does denote such a two-place relation, then whatever is thought of must be something, even if it does not exist. I can think of Spider-Man – maybe I do this too often – and so Spider-Man is something I stand in a relation to. But Spider-Man is something I stand in a relation to only if Spider-Man is something. So, Spider-Man is something. (As we'll see in Section 1.2.3, the argument is often attributed to Meinong, but it is only one element in his case for nonexistent objects.)

Let's take a step back. "Whether there are things that don't exist" is akin to other metaphysical questions such as the following:

Q1: Are there things that are not concrete?
Q2: Are there things that are not particulars?
Q3: Are there things that are not present?
Q4: Are there things that are not actual?

Does assimilating the big question to these questions presuppose that the big question is conceptually open in the way that – perhaps to varying degrees – these questions here are conceptually open? Platonists and nominalists debate Q1, and it seems that few nominalists think that a negative answer to Q1 is mandated by our concepts.[9] Similar remarks apply to Q2. With respect to Q3 and Q4, we do find some philosophers arguing that negative answers are conceptually mandated: certain presentists or actualists think that it is conceptually necessary that everything is present or actual.[10] With respect to Q3, one putative reason for claiming that a negative answer is conceptually mandated is that the verb "are" appearing in Q3 is present-tensed but there is no "untensed" conjugation of this verb that could be used to state a meaningful version of Q3 that could be nontrivially affirmatively answered. With respect to Q4, one putative reason for claiming that a negative answer is conceptually mandated is that "actual" is redundant: To say that a proposition is actually true is just to say that a proposition is true, and to say that there is an actual entity that is a certain way is just to say that there is an entity that is that way.

Similarly, perhaps nonexistent objects are conceptually impossible. Suppose that existence reduces to quantification: To say that dogs exist, for example, is just to say that there are dogs, and to say that I exist is just to say that something is identical with me. If existence reduces to quantification in this way, then the claim that there are nonexistent objects just is the claim that there are things such that there are no such things. And that claim is logically incoherent! It seems then that nonexistent objects are conceptually possible only if existence is not reducible to quantification.

In contemporary metaphysics, the dominant view is still that existence reduces to quantification. But in the history of philosophy, this view is decidedly in the minority. For example, in Novotný's (2013) masterful study of late

---

[9] Although for a view in the neighborhood of this claim, see Hofweber (2016).
[10] For a discussion of the claim that presentism is trivially true, see Ludlow (2004); for a discussion of whether possibilism is conceptually incoherent, see Lycan (1988).

scholastic views about beings of reason, Novotný (2013: 29) notes that for the scholastics, existence and being are not the same: "exists" is a first-order predicate not reducible to the quantifier, and it denotes a nontrivial property that some but not all items enjoy. The question of whether there are things that don't exist is by their lights conceptually open, and given this, it is unsurprising to find a range of opinions on this question expressed.

Perhaps a quick dip into some of the history of the problem of nonexistents will be helpful.

1.2 Some Dead People on Nonexistent Objects

I will not pretend that this section is comprehensive. Instead, I will discuss how the problem of nonexistents was addressed by a select few historical figures at certain points in their philosophical journeys. Still, a scattershot survey of this sort can be useful even if all that it does prevents contemporary philosophers from thinking that the problem of nonexistence has its origins in the early part of the twentieth century.

One reason why the problem of nonexistents was so thorny in the history of philosophy is that for many philosophers, the idea of being is itself not particularly straightforward. Aristotle said that "being is said in many ways," and although what exactly he meant by this is contested, it seems that the way in which a substance is "said to be" is not the same as the ways in which members of other ontological categories are "said to be."[11] Does Aristotle's claim imply that "being" is semantically ambiguous? Or does it imply that there are modes of being? Are both of these implied?[12] (Ontological pluralism will be discussed more in Section 2.7.)

Regardless, according to Aristotle, even nonexistent objects can, in some way, be said to be – and in fact, there must be a way in which they can be said to be, since we can say true things about them. (Just as one might wonder whether "thought of" is a two-place relation between a thinker and a thing, one might wonder whether "about" is a two-place relation between a truth and a thing.) Even nonbeing itself can in some way be said to be![13]

What is it to exist? We might provisionally reserve the word "exist" for things that can truthfully be said to be in the way that we can truthfully be said to be. On this usage, we exist, plants exist, but nonbeing does not exist. However, according to a strict Aristotelian, given this usage, properties, relations, events,

---

[11] See Aristotle's *Metaphysics* IV.2, 1003a33–b19.
[12] See McDaniel (2017: Introduction and chapter 1) for a tentative presentation of an ontologically pluralist reading of Aristotle, and Czerkawski (2022) for a critical response to one argument for attributing ontological pluralism to Aristotle.
[13] See Aristotle's *Metaphysics* 1003b10.

and so on do not exist either. A broader proposal is that something exists if and only if it belongs to one of the Aristotelian categories.[14] On this proposal, you exist, and so do your properties, but none of nonbeing, blindness in an eye, or centaurs exist. Given this proposal, we could safely attribute the claim that there are nonexistent objects to those historical figures who follow Aristotle's doctrine of the categories so understood. One such figure is Suarez, to whom we now turn.

1.2.1 Suarez

Although beings of reason, which our provisional understanding of "existence" classifies as nonexistents, had been previously theorized about, it is in the hands of Suarez that they first receive a thorough examination. Suarez devoted an entire investigation (specifically, #54!) of his lengthy tome to the status and nature of beings of reason. In what follows, I will cover some of this investigation's highlights.

Suarez (Section 1, paragraph 6) begins by clarifying the concept of a being of reason. According to Suarez, what is rightfully defined as a being of reason is that which has being only objectively in the intellect, or that which is thought by reason as a being, even though "it has no entity in itself."[15] Suarez notes that Aquinas says that a being of reason is produced at the moment when an intellect tries to apprehend what is not and then fashions it in some manner as being.

So, what is it to think of something "by reason as a being"? One plausible answer is that it is to judge something about it. When I judge that the blindness in my eye is getting worse, I treat the blindness in my eye as the *object* of the judgment – it is what the judgment is about. When I do this, at least as far as the power of judgment is concerned, the blindness in my eye is treated as an object just as much as any other object. Just as I can judge that the blindness in my eye is getting worse, I can judge that my headache is getting worse. Just as I can judge that the hole in the road is getting wider, I can judge that my belly is getting wider. From the perspective of the faculty of judgment, all of these objects are available to judge.

That beings of reason are produced via judgments about them is suggested by Suarez's (Section 2, paragraphs 15–17) remarks that a being of reason "properly comes to be through that act of the intellect by which something that in reality has no entity is conceived in the manner of a being." We are told that this act of the intellect is a comparative or reflexive act, that is, an act that presupposes

---

[14] Or is God – traditionally, if God can be said to belong to a category, it is a category consisting of only God.
[15] See Novotný (2013: 48–50) for careful discussion of the idea of being objectively in an intellect.

other mental activities.[16] A judgment is a paradigmatic reflexive act, since I can form a judgment only if other mental activities have already produced the materials from which to make that judgment. Moreover, Suarez claims that a being of reason arises "only through the intellect" because neither sense nor will can produce them, and that's because neither of these faculties has the power to "conceive of something not truly a being in the manner of a being."

But can't I *see* a hole? Or *want* an absence of something? If I can plan to blind someone, can't I thereby will that he has blindness in his eye? Moreover, I don't know if Suarez credits animals with having the faculty of an intellect, but it does seem like they try to avoid falling into holes.

Although beings of reason have no "entity in themselves" – they aren't real, existent things – there are such things. However, Suarez takes such things to be mind-dependent, and this is part of what is entailed by saying that they have being only objectively in the intellect. Where there are no existing intellects, there would also be no nonexistent entities. Later proponents of nonexistent things, such as Meinong, will disagree sharply with Suarez here; on, for example, Meinong's view, a nonexistent round square would be an object even if there were no existing things thinking about – and even if there were no existing things at all. (We will see that Meinong also thinks that we *see* some nonexistent objects as well!)

Perhaps the following argument is why Suarez thought that beings of reason were mind-dependent. Let's consider a particular being of reason, such as the hole in the left sock that I am currently wearing. Necessarily, there is an object that is this hole only if this hole has being objectively in the intellect. But, necessarily, this hole has being objectively in the intellect only if there is a judgment made about this hole. However, necessarily, there is a judgment made about this hole only if there is a mind making that judgment. It follows then that, necessarily, there is an object such as this hole only if there is a mind that makes a judgment about this hole.

This is a very strong form of mind-dependence. Perhaps it is too strong, and if so, the argument just made must have a false premise.[17] For what it's worth, it does seem strange to me that holes are partially created by making judgments about them, since it seems that holes can be discovered and then judged about. Didn't I first see the hole in my sock and then later form a judgment about it? Perhaps Suarez would respond that I first saw that my sock was perforated, and

---

[16] See Novotný (2013: 73–74) for discussion of the idea of reflexive act, though I do not see Novotný as identifying these acts with judgments.

[17] In McDaniel (2017: 153–154), I argue against the claim that holes are judgment (or mind, more generally) dependent in this way.

then judged that it had a hole in it. Perhaps this is correct, but this putative response seems somewhat contrived.

Suarez (paragraph 8) then turns to the question of why beings of reason are "contrived." He offers three accounts of why we make judgments about beings of reason. We are interested in negations and privations, but we must think of them as beings; we have imperfect insight (at best) into the intrinsic natures of things, and so must think of things in terms of relations, many of which are relations of reason; and our imagination runs wild and we construct impossible figments. In each case, a cognitive deficiency or imperfection in us is a crucial part of the explanation for why beings of reason are "contrived." A perfect being needn't think of negations or privations as beings, and would have perfect insight into the natures of things, and presumably it would neither have nor need a faculty of imagination that would run wild in the way ours does.

The role of the imagination in "contriving" beings of reason complicates the earlier claim about judgment.[18] Suarez does seem to say (Section 2, paragraph 18) that imagination forms by beings of reason by combining simple images, and that some philosophers ("dialecticians") hold that the beings thereby contrived need not be possible beings. On the face of it, the claim that beings of reason are formed by imagination is incompatible with the claim that beings of reason are always formed by acts of the intellect, since the intellect seems as distinct of a faculty from the imagination as it does from the faculties of sense and will. But maybe there is a way to thread the needle here. Let's consider an example. Suppose I have a mental image of a horse and a mental image of a horn. I then use my imagination to construct a more complex image. I have not yet "contrived" a being of reason, however, for I have not yet used this more complex image as the basis of a judgment, as I do when I judge that this is an image *of* a unicorn. When I make this final step, I thereby treat what is not in itself a being as a being.

Suarez claims that beings of reason have being objectively in the intellect. This claim raises the question, whose intellect? Consider again the hole in my sock. As far as I know, I am the only one who knows about it. So, it seems that the hole in my sock has being objectively in my intellect, but perhaps not in anyone else's intellect. But does this imply that if I were to die, the hole would no longer in any sense be? And if so, what happens when someone else discovers my sock? Is it numerically the same hole that once had being objectively in my intellect but that now has being objectively in someone else's? Or is it a numerically different hole? Neither option seems particularly appealing.

---

[18] As astutely noted in Novotný (2013: 74–76).

Probably this particular worry would disappear if that hole always has being objectively in someone's intellect, at least for as long as intuitively the hole is at all. And Suarez suggests (section 23) that this is the case. There, he raises and affirmatively answers the question of whether beings of reason have being objectively in the Divine Intellect, even though God doesn't "contrive" beings of reasons.[19] If the hole in the sock has being objectively in God's intellect, then it doesn't cease to be when I die, and so it needn't return when someone else discovers it. Much like Berkeley's God, who is always observing the quad, Suarez's God has a lock on the hole in my sock.

However, the claim that beings of reason have being objectively in God's intellect raises several hard questions. Recall that we contrive beings of reason because we are cognitively imperfect – and so understandably Suarez (Section 2, paragraph 19–23) argues that God, who is a perfect being, doesn't contrive beings of reason. But how can something merely have being objectively in a mind if it is not contrived by that mind? Consider the hole in my sock. No one besides me (and maybe God) has judged anything about it, including my neighbors across the street. Does the hole in the sock nonetheless have being objectively in their intellects? If we sever the connection between contriving a being of reason and its having being objectively in an intellect, we will be hard-pressed to explain why the hole my sock doesn't have being objectively in their intellects. But we will also be hard-pressed to explain why the being that a hole in the sock has is mere being objectively in an intellect as opposed to a mind-independent kind of being.

Suppose the hole in my sock has being objectively in the mind of God. When did it acquire this status? There are two plausible options. First, it acquired this status when the sock it resides in first became perforated. Second, it acquired this status when I formed a judgment about the hole. The first option seems more plausible – recall the earlier question about whether I discover a hole in my sock, and then later form a judgment about that hole. Moreover, if the hole in my sock acquires being objectively in God's intellect only after I have judged something about this hole, it seems that God is subject to change. But is God subject to change? On the other hand, if the first option is true, it seems that I do not contrive the hole in my sock. And since God doesn't contrive it either, it seems that it has a kind of being independent of whether an intellect makes a judgment about it.

As we will see, later proponents of nonexistent objects completely dissociate the presence of such objects with their being judged about.

---

[19] See also Novotný (2013: 76–79) for a discussion of God and beings of reason.

1.2.2 Kazimierz Twardowski

Although Meinong is the most famous defender of nonexistent objects, one of his contemporaries, Twardowski, deserves his place in the sun as well. This section will focus on the fifth chapter of his 1894 book *On the Content and Object of Presentations*, which is titled, "On Act, Content, and Object."

There are three items referred to in this chapter's title. The act is the mental act, that is, the product of mental activity. A judgment is an act in this sense, since it is the product of the activity judging. A presentation is also an act.

What about "content"? This technical phrase ("Inhalt") and analogous phrases were highly scrutinized during this time period. Some took the content of an act to be more mental stuff, and so understood the contents of acts to be genuine parts of the acts. Husserl, for example, sometimes spoke of the "hyle" or the "matter" of a mental act.[20] For Husserl, sense data often was the matter of mental acts. But another possibility is that the content of an act is *the sense* of the act, which would not be a real part of the mental act, but rather an *aspect* of the act that can be instantiated by numerically distinct acts. This seems to be what Twardowski has in mind.[21]

The object of an act is that to which the act refers, and it is never a part of the act that refers to it. Twardowski claims that every mental act has an object, and much of chapter 5 focuses on defending this claim. He takes the key question to be whether there are objectless presentations, and since he claims that Bolzano had claimed that there were, Twardowski works through Bolzano's alleged examples.

The first example suggested by Bolzano is the presentation that corresponds to the word "nothing." Since no object is denoted by this word, the corresponding presentation is also without an object. Twardowski grants that there is no such object as nothing. However, Twardowski also denies that "nothing" corresponds to a presentation. Instead, according to Twardowski, "nothing" seems to be a syncategorematic expression, rather than one that attempts to denote something. (Presumably, there is neither a presentation nor an object corresponding to "and" either.)

The second example suggested by Bolzano is the presentation that corresponds to the phrase, "oblique square." Twardoswki grants that no oblique square exists, but then insists that only as an object of a presentation can the existence of an oblique square be denied. He warns us not to confuse the

---

[20] See Husserl (2005a: 213–215). Husserl (2005b: 165) sometimes uses "representative content" to designate the sensory component of a perception; Husserl (1982: 205) also uses the phrase "hyletic data."

[21] See, for example, page 21, where he says that the content of an act is the meaning of a corresponding name.

nonexistence of an object with its not being presented, since the former does not imply the latter. Being presented is not a way of existing (p. 22), and so an object can be presented even if it does not exist.

Twardowski does not demand sole credit for these claims. On the contrary, according to Twardowski (pp. 22–23), Descartes also held that every presentation presents an object. Materially true presentations present existent objects; materially false presentations present nonexistent ones.

However, Twardowski acknowledges that there is a serious worry for his view that is generated by judgments about relations. Twardowski accepts Brentano's theory of existential judgments, according to which these judgments are not propositional attitudes but rather object-directed attitudes that affirm the object in question.[22] Consider the difference between these assertions.

A1: I love the twenty-first-century Monads.

A2: I love that the twenty-first-century Monads are releasing a new album in 2026.

A2 expresses a propositional attitude. When someone asserts A2, they are indicating that they love *that something is the case*. However, A1 does not express a propositional attitude; instead, when someone asserts A1, they indicate that they love *a particular object*, in this case, a musical group. It is far from obvious that the object-directed attitude expressed by A1 in some way reduces to a propositional attitude.

For Brentano, when I say "O exists," what I express is not a belief directed toward a proposition. Rather, what I express is an affirmation of the object itself. Existential judgment is an object-directed attitude.[23] Similarly, a denial of existence is a rejection of an object. Moreover, according to Brentano, *all* judgments at rock bottom are existential judgments (or denials of existence). Twardowski calls this the "idiogenetic theory of judgment."

Brentano endorsed this theory partly because it enabled him to dispense with abstract propositions when characterizing the nature of judgment.[24] And Twardowski is inclined to accept the idiogenetic theory. So, let's assess why Twardowski thinks that judgments about relations are troublesome for this theory. Suppose I judge truly that Sam is wiser than Kris. According to the idiogenetic theory, what I am doing is affirming an object: the particular relation of superior wisdom of Sam over Kris. Let's call this particular relation, "R."

---

[22] See Kriegel (2017) for a nice overview of Brentano's theory of judgment. Note that Brentano prefers a theory in which *all* judgments are (positive or negative) existential judgments; my focus here is on Brentano's theory of existential judgment, and not on the thesis that all judgments are existential judgments.

[23] See again Kriegel (2017, section 3).   [24] See Kriegel (2017, section 1).

Since my judgment is true, R can be correctly affirmed. Here is the kind of argument that Twardowski is worried about:

1. Necessarily, one can affirm R only if one also affirms Sam and affirms Kris.[25]
2. If 1, then one can correctly affirm R only if one can correctly affirm Sam and Kris.
3. So, one can correctly affirm R only if one can correctly affirm Sam and Kris.
4. One can correctly affirm R.
5. So, one can correctly affirm Sam and Kris.
6. If 5, then Sam and Kris both exist.

So, Sam and Kris both exist.

This particular argument happens to have a true conclusion, but that's not what is at issue. The issue is that *whenever* one can correctly affirm a relation, it thereby follows that its relata exist, contrary to Twardowski's view that non-existents can stand in relation to each other, and to existent things. Consider a parallel argument about Samwise and Frodo – and let R* be the particular relation of greater wisdom of Samwise to Frodo.

1. Necessarily, one can affirm R* only if one also affirms Samwise and Frodo.
2. If 1, then one can correctly affirm R* only if one can correctly affirm Samwise and Frodo.
3. So, one can correctly affirm R* only if one can correctly affirm Samwise and Frodo.
4. One can correctly affirm R*.
5. So, one can correctly affirm Samwise and Frodo.
6. If 5, then Samwise and Frodo both exist.

So, Samwise and Frodo both exist.

In light of this argument, one might expect Twardowski to either reject outright or at least revise the idiogenetic theory of judgment. One possible revision is to deny that an existential judgment about an ordinary object such as a cat is simply an affirmation of that object. Instead, one could hold that it is affirmation of the particular existence of that cat. One could then introduce a notion of a presentational judgment, which one makes when one affirms that Samwise is an object. (A presentational judgment about an object might be expressed in language via a sentence that begins with a name for that object followed by "is something.") Given Twardowski's views, all presentational

---

[25] This seems suggested by Brentano's (1995: 208) remarks to the effect that whenever one affirms a combination, one thereby also affirms each of the elements in that combination.

judgments so understood are true, but not all existential judgments would be, since some things would have no aspect of existence to affirm.

Another possibility is to simply take presentational affirmation and existential affirmation to be distinct object-oriented attitudes, irreducible to one another. On this view, "affirming an object" is ambiguous between these two attitudes, and so the argument presented here is also ambiguous.[26]

True, a necessary condition on existentially affirming an object is to presentationally affirm that object. But it is also a necessary condition that one must have a presentation of an object in order to existentially affirm it. This suggests a simpler theory: a presentational affirmation of an object is just a presentation of that object. This simpler theory also explains why it is trivial that all presentational affirmations of objects are correct. Hume thought that the idea of an object is always an idea of it as an existing object.[27] On this modified version of Twardowksi's view, Hume's thought is not correct, since one can have an idea of an object without seeing it as existing. However, something like Hume's view is right for *being something*. To have a presentation of a thing just is to see it as being something, which in turn is also a way of affirming the thing.

Twardowski seems to reject premise 1 of this argument, though it is hard to figure out exactly why. The main gist seems to be that since Samwise and Frodo are not the subjects of the sentence affirming the existence of a relation between them, their existence is not thereby implicated as well. (See the remarks on Poseidon at the end of chapter 5.) Perhaps one oddity of this response is that a relation can exist even though none of the relata that it in fact relates exist.

1.2.3 Meinong

We turn next to Meinong, whose embrace of the nonexistent was so notorious that the doctrine that there are nonexistent objects is now named after him. Meinong had two motivations for believing in nonexistent objects. The first is phenomenological. According to Meinong (1904: 76), "that judgments or presentations are impossible without being judgments about or presentations of something, is revealed to be self-evident by a quite elementary examination of these experiences." Some nonexistent objects are presented to us intellectually, such as the round square. But other nonexistent objects are presented to

---

[26] This view is actually suggested by Lotze (1884: 439), who writes, "when we call anything Real, we mean always to affirm it, though in different senses according to the different forms which it assumes, but one or other of which it must necessarily assume, and of which no one is reducible to or contained in the other. For we never can get an Event out of simple Being, the reality which belongs to Things, namely Being or Existence, never belongs to Events – they do not exist but occur; again a Proposition neither exists like things nor occurs like events; that its meaning even obtains like a relation, can only be said if the things exist of which it predicates a relation."
[27] See Hume (1978: 66–67).

us in perception! For example, Meinong (1904: 83–85) argues that we see colors, but also that colors do not exist. He seems in this case to be persuaded by the empiricists' worries about secondary qualities; Meinong grants that some properties, for example, the shape of a book, might subsist – that is, enjoy the mode of being that is peculiar to abstracta – but others, such as the blueness of this Element, are objects that neither exist nor subsist. In this respect, Meinong might differ from some of his predecessors, such as Suarez, who seemed to think that the only way we recognize beings of reason is intellectually (and perhaps imaginatively), but we never literally see them.

Meinong's second motivation was theoretical, and this motivation will be the focus of my discussion here. As many philosophers were at the time, Meinong was concerned about how to properly demarcate the different sciences of the day, with special concern about how psychology, logic, mathematics, and metaphysics related to one another. The key to seeing how these disciplines are related is to develop a maximally comprehensive science, Meinong's Theory of Objects.

The Theory of Objects is intended to be maximally comprehensive in two ways. First, every object is included in its subject matter, regardless of whether it exists, subsists, or fails to be either. Second, it states a priori universal principles applying to all objects regardless of what kind of object they might be.[28] Here are some of the principles that are included among the Theory: every object has properties; every object is such that there is a true objective (for our purposes, consider these to be propositions) about it; if an object has inconsistent properties, it neither exists nor subsists.

Admittedly, principles of this sort seem somewhat thin, and if the Theory of Objects merely consisted of them, it would not be particularly impressive. However, Meinong (1904: 98–99) subsumes all of pure mathematics as a subfield of the Theory of Objects. Meinong (1904: 81) argues that if there are only things that exist, then every science must either be a science of the mind (and so a part of psychology) or a science of nature, for example, physics or chemistry. But mathematics is neither a science of the mind nor a science of nature. So, either mathematics is not a science at all or there must be more objects than merely those that exist. Since the former disjunct is false, there are nonexistent objects.

Meinong (1904: 101–103) distinguishes two ways of doing philosophy of science. The first is "the natural approach," in which we theorize about already existing sciences. The second approach is *anticipatory*: We determine which

---

[28] In this respect, Meinong's Theory of Objects is akin to Husserl's project of a formal ontology, which was initially proposed in his third logical investigation; see Husserl 2005b, Investigation Three.

sciences do not exist but *should*, and we do this by seeing the natural ways of gathering objects into groupings and propositions into systems of principles. The Theory of Objects subsumes mathematics in a way analogous to how mathematical sciences subsume other fields. Consider, for example, the expansion of geometry originally conceived as the science of physical space to a more abstract conception in which geometrical relations such as distance can now relate things like "points of colour" in "colour space." The subject matter of geometry so understood has been broadened so that it is about a plethora of topic-neutral relations that can be studied regardless of what they are applied to.

How do psychology, epistemology, and logic relate to the Theory of Objects? Meinong denies that psychology subsumes the Theory of Objects, although he notes that one might initially think that it does. According to Meinong, all psychological states are intentional, that is, have what Meinong (1904: 87) calls "objectivity."[29] Meinong prefers the technical term "objectivity" rather than "intentionality" because for a state to be intentional for Meinong is for it to correspond to an object that is numerically distinct from that state. (This is not the case for Husserl or later Brentano.) So, it is natural to think that since the subject matter of psychology is states that have objects, psychology is also the science best suited to study the objects themselves. As Meinong puts it (ibid), "For the science which most naturally would have to deal with objects as such would be the very one whose business it is to deal with the Objectivity. This task ... seems to belong to psychology." Moreover, Meinong (1904: 87–88) suggests that "the current direction of psychology" is one that studies both psychological states and their correlated objects, and cites the psychology of sound and color as evidence of this trend, since these branches of psychology must study sounds and colors themselves in order to investigate our experiences of sounds and colors.

However, the fact that psychology is the science of objectivity does not show that psychology is suited to be the science of objects. Psychology can deal with objects only insofar as they are actually presented – but Meinong (1904: 90) claims that the plurality of objects goes beyond this. And we can consider how these objects are independent of their presentation in psychological states. This is true even of colors, for example, which stand in quasi-geometrical relations to one another (think of the color wheel) independent of whether they exist or are represented by us.

The theory of objects is not subsumed by psychology. Moreover, Meinong believes that the theory of objects also shows us why epistemology is not

---

[29] Meinong is following his teacher, Brentano (1995) here, who claimed that intentionality is what distinguishes psychological phenomena from physical phenomena.

subsumable by psychology either. Recall that all psychological states are directed toward objects. Meinong (1904: 95–96) considers the following dilemma: either the object to which a psychological state is directed exists in reality or it exists entirely "in my idea," that is, is mind-dependent, and in which case is the proper object of study of psychologists. The former disjunct is ruled out by innumerable examples in which we think of things that do not or cannot exist in reality. The latter disjunct is psychologistic in the bad sense, since objects such as the round square do not exist "in my idea" of them. Meinong suspects that it is a prejudice in favor of the actual that generates this false dilemma. But another possibility is that because every object corresponds to at least one true objective, and an objective is true if and only if it subsists, one might mistakenly think that every object at least inherits subsistence from the true objectives about it.

But the ignoring of objectives is itself a damaging error. Suppose that one forgets that there are objectives, but remembers correctly that knowledge is always, in a sense, knowledge of something real. Then one will think that knowledge is always of real objects, and hence either there are no non-real objects or non-real objects cannot be known. But the object of knowledge strictly speaking is always a (subsisting) objective, rather than an object that is not also an objective. When I know that the table is in the room, the object of my knowledge is the subsisting objective *that the table is in the room* rather than a table or a chair. Similarly, when I know that the round square is impossible, the object of my knowledge is the subsisting objective *that the round square is impossible* rather than the round square, which neither exists nor subsists.

Meinong diagnoses the temptation to psychologism in epistemology as ultimately stemming from ignoring both objects and objectives. But the Theory of Objects prevents us from making this mistake, and thereby paves the way for the development of a well-founded epistemology. And, for this reason, the Theory of Objects is not subsumed by epistemology, since it is needed to help decide the correct epistemology.

Finally, let's turn to logic. As already noted, the status of logic and its relation to psychology was one of the thorniest questions of the late nineteenth and early twentieth centuries. Both Frege (1980) and Husserl (2005a) were fierce opponents of reducing logic to psychology. Meinong's conception of logic is more psychologistic than theirs, but his Theory of Objects is also relevantly similar to Husserl's project of formal ontology, which Husserl conceived to be a part of logic.

According to Husserl (2005b: 68–69), one of the tasks of pure logic is to fix the "pure categories of meaning," which include *concept, proposition, and truth*. Another task of pure logic is to fix the *pure, formal categories of object*, which include Object, State of Affairs, Unity, Plurality, Relation, Number, Connection, and so on.[30] Husserl's goal is to determine the "phenomenological origin" of the concepts of these categories, which requires us to figure out the original intuitions in which the objects of these concepts were first presented.

Meinong says that he agrees with Husserl's attacks on *psychologism*, which were stimulated by Frege's (1972) review of Husserl's previous book. But Meinong is hesitant to classify his project as "pure logic," because he worries that logic is fundamentally a *practical* endeavor, "devoted to the advancement" of our intellectual powers. Meinong (pp. 93–94) also worries that some of the concepts Husserl discusses are in fact psychological concepts and not concepts belonging to the theory of objects proper. Meinong suggests that logic can't fully extricate itself from practical/normative psychological concerns, and that even the terminology of logic suggests this. What makes something a proposition is that it is the sort of the thing that can be proposed, as it were, and this is a psychological notion. If the study of inference is part of the study of logic, as it seems to be, this too is an invasion of psychology – since patterns of inference are the psychological analogue of patterns of circulation of blood in an organism.

However, Meinong (1904: 93–95) also suggests that this dissent with Husserl is "minor" and might be terminological. Most importantly, Meinong agrees that two distinctions are important: the distinction between *content* and object, and the distinction between object and objective. The *content* of an intentional state is not the object represented by that state, but rather is a genuine part of the intentional state itself. Contents so understood are always existing objects even though the objects that correspond to contents might not exist.

To sum up, Meinong's reasons for endorsing Meinongianism were not merely phenomenological but also theoretical. Nonexistent objects provide the subject matter for a rich Theory of Objects, whose existence clarifies how extant disciplines stand to each other. Meinong's objects do theoretical work.

As we will see in the next section, some contemporary philosophers invoke Meinongianism, or something like it, because of the work that this theory can do for them. With this in mind, we leave the history of metaontology and return to the present age.

1.3 A Contemporary Application of Meinongianism

One of the most prominent Meinongians, although he prefers the label "noneist," also embraces nonexistent objects partly because they are theoretically useful. Priest (2005) argues that nonexistent objects provide the resources for

---
[30] See Husserl (2005b: 72–73).

a proper theory of intentional sentential operators. Here is some of the background to this idea. David Lewis (1986) argued for an ontology of possible worlds because such an ontology is theoretically fruitful. Part of its theoretical fruitfulness is that modal operators – a small subset of intentional operators – can be understood as quantifiers over possible worlds, which in turn clarifies their logical properties. Lewis thought that these non-actual worlds all existed; Priest disagrees here, claiming that no non-actual world exists even though there are many such worlds. And in way, Priest goes further by claiming that there are nonexistent impossible worlds as well. This richer framework of worlds allows for a richer set of reductive analyses not possible in Lewis's system.

Consider *belief*. I believe many things, such as that 7 + 5 = 12, that the sky is blue, and that the authoritarian threat to democracy needs to be addressed head on. Some of my beliefs are what I believe is merely contingently true, while others are necessarily true. Focus on beliefs about matters that are contingent. Here is a natural, but not mandatory, model of belief: When one believes, one locates oneself in a sphere of possible worlds that are consistent with what one believes.[31] A toy illustration of this model: early in life, I am a blank slate – I have had no experience, and so I do not exclude any possible worlds as ones that I am not located at. I acquire some experience – I see that the sky is blue. Now I place myself in a sphere of possible worlds at which the sky is blue. As I acquire further beliefs about contingent matters, this sphere shrinks. To be maximally opinionated about contingent matters is to locate oneself in exactly one possible world. To be omniscient with respect to contingent truths is to know exactly what world one is in. This model mode suggests a reduction of the intentional operator of belief to a universal quantifier over possible worlds: to believe that P is for P to be true at all of the worlds in the sphere in which I locate myself.

This model does fairly well with contingent beliefs, although there is at least one hiccup: on this model, if I believe that P, I believe all that is entailed by P. Suppose I believe that P, and that Q is entailed by P. Since I believe P, P is true at all of the worlds in the sphere in which I locate myself. Since P entails Q, Q is also true at all of the worlds in the sphere in which I locate myself. But then, given this model, I believe Q as well. That's surprising, but worse is to come: since every necessary truth is entailed by any proposition, it follows that from the fact that I believe P, which is a contingent truth, I thereby believe all the necessary truths. This doesn't seem plausible. So, it looks as though, even if modal operators like "necessarily" reduce to (or at least can be modeled by)

---

[31] This is roughly like the account of belief defended in Lewis (1986: section 1.4).

quantification over possible worlds, other intentional operators resist such a treatment.

Enter impossible worlds. Suppose that P is contingent, that P entails Q, and that I have no opinion about Q. Although there is no possible world at which P and not-Q are both true, there are nonetheless worlds in which P and not-Q are both true. And since I have no opinion about P, I locate myself in a sphere of worlds that includes some P and Q worlds and some P and not-Q worlds. Belief can be understood in terms of universal quantification, provided that the domain includes impossible worlds.

An impossible world seems like a paradigmatic example of a thing that cannot, and so does not, exist. There are treatments of impossible worlds on which these things do exist. But if the best theory of impossible worlds is a theory on which they are nonexistent, and if impossible worlds are theoretically useful, we have a pragmatic reason to traffic in them, much like the pragmatic reason Lewis offered for trafficking in possible worlds.[32]

In general, the putative theoretical usefulness of nonexistent objects is a challenge for foes of nonexistent objects. They need to show that either the jobs nonexistent objects are called to do are not needed to be done or that the jobs can be done by existent objects instead.

1.4 Zalta's Object Theory

Suppose that there are nonexistent objects. This supposition leaves it open what they are like. According to many friends of the nonexistent, expressions such as "the round square" and "the golden mountain" denote nonexistent objects; let's assume they do. So, is the round square round? (And square?) Is the golden mountain a mountain? There seems some pressure to answer "yes," for if the round square weren't round, and the golden mountain weren't a mountain, why would we call them that? The *characterization postulate* is the claim that whenever a predicate appears as part of a definite description that denotes something, that predicate is true of the object. The characterization postulate implies that the golden mountain is a mountain.

But it seems that the characterization postulate has counterexamples. Consider the description "the existent round square." Suppose that this denotes an object. It must be round and square, but also exist! Perhaps "the existent round square" doesn't denote – but then why believe that "the round square" does? So, it seems that either some denoting phrases do not denote or the characterization principle must be replaced with something less permissive.

---

[32] See also Yagisawa (2009) for an argument for impossible worlds.

Metaontology 21

But perhaps there is a third option. One of Meinong's students, Ernst Mally (1912), argued that we need to distinguish two ways in which a predicate might be true of an object – or, better put perhaps, two ways in which a property might be had by an object: the property might be *exemplified* by the object or it might be *encoded* by the object. The golden mountain is a mountain – but it only encodes the property of being a mountain, unlike Mount Everest, which exemplifies this property.

More recently, Mally's idea has been defended by Ed Zalta (2006), and incorporated in his object theory.[33] Zalta's object theory doesn't distinguish between quantification and existence, but does hold that some concrete things could have existed without being concrete. I suspect that Zalta's theory is merely terminologically different from a theory in which the contingently nonconcrete are nonexistent objects. But let's explore the theory first. Here are its relevant components.

First, everything exists necessarily, although many of what necessarily exists is only contingently concrete. Socrates is a necessary existent who is contingently concrete. Included in what necessarily exists are abstract objects, which are also necessary nonconcrete.[34] Hence, the distinction between concrete objects and abstract objects is not an exhaustive distinction, since a merely possibly concrete object is not an abstract object.

Second, there are two fundamentally different modes of predication or ways in which an object can "have" a property.[35] Sherlock Holmes exists and is a detective, but he does not *exemplify* being a detective, unlike one of my neighbors who is a concrete detective for the local police force. Rather, Sherlock Holmes, who is an abstract rather than concrete object, *encodes* being a detective. It seems to be part of Zalta's (2006: 663) theory of objects that such abstract objects encode all and only those properties that are inherent in our conceptions of them.

Third, as a matter of necessity, the only objects that encode properties are abstract objects.[36] Things that are or could be concrete never encode but always exemplify properties.

The first two parts of the system are independently motivated. The first part is motivated by virtue of being a consequence of the simplest version of quantified

---

[33] Mally distinguished the *determination* of an object by a property and the *satisfaction* of that property by an object. See Zalta (1998) for a discussion of Mally, along with translations of some of the relevant texts. Mally's theory was developed in the context of thinking through Meinong's theory of objects, which included nonexistent objects such as *the round square*. See also McMichael and Zalta (1980).

[34] See Linsky and Zalta (1994, 1996). Also relevant is Williamson (2013).

[35] See McMichael and Zalta (1980) and Zalta (1992, 1995, & 2006).

[36] See Zalta (1992: 61, 1995: 194, & 2006: 662, 678).

modal logic.[37] The second part is motivated by traditional concerns about putative nonexistent objects, such as creatures of fiction and myth. But why accept the third component?

Plausibly, the nature of a nonexistent object is exhausted by the properties that they encode; these properties constitute its *essence* in the strict sense. The essence of a thing in this strict sense is not simply the collection of features it exemplifies as a matter of necessity. (As Fine (1994) argued, it is not part of my essence that I am a member of my singleton set, although I am a member of it as a matter of necessity.) It is of the essence of the golden mountain that it encodes being a mountain. Here is a hypothesis: In general, an object encodes a property if and only if it is a part of its essence. However, this hypothesis is incompatible with Zalta's third component.

There are three options. First, scrap the idea of an essence in the strict sense. Second, take the notion of an essence in the strict sense as an additional primitive, over and above the primitives of encoding and exemplifying. (Accordingly, essentially having a property would be a third way of having a property.) Third, give a reductive account of essence in terms of other aspects of the theory.

Zalta (2006: 678, 691) pursues the third option and provides a disjunctive theory of essence: What it is for a property to be essential to an object depends on whether the object is an abstract object or a possibly concrete object. A feature F is essential to an abstract object just in case, necessarily, it encodes F. For possibly concrete objects, Zalta (2006: 679) distinguishes between weak and strong essential features. A feature F is weakly essential to a possibly concrete object just in case, necessarily, if it is concrete, it exemplifies F. A feature F is strongly essential to a possibly concrete object just in case F is weakly essential to it but it is not the case that it necessarily exemplifies F. Being a member of his singleton set is not strongly essential to Socrates, for although it is weakly essential to him, Socrates belongs to that set necessarily. Recall that Socrates necessarily exists but is only contingently concrete. In every world, Socrates is a member of his singleton set, even those worlds in which he is nonconcrete. Similarly, Socrates is weakly essentially not identical with Kit Fine, but he also is necessarily not Kit Fine, and hence Socrates is not strongly essentially not identical with Kit Fine.

Although it looks initially promising, the theory is subject to counterexamples. Wildman (2016: 186) considers being human and that the Eiffel tower is essentially a tower. This is a property that is strongly essential to Socrates (given Zalta's definitions), but is intuitively not essential to Socrates. Wildman (2016:

---

[37] See Linsky and Zalta (1996).

186–190) considers a series of ways of modifying Zalta's theory in light of even more counterexamples, but Wildman (216: 188) notes that the final theory he arrives at is "a terribly complicated definition, which manages to avoid counterexamples only via the accumulation of gerrymandered, ad hoc restrictions." Since I share Wildman's judgment here, I will refrain from tediously documenting the epicycles.

As already noted, Zalta denies that possibly concrete objects encode properties. On the theory considered here, possibly concrete objects encode properties as well as exemplify them. Moreover, we accept Zalta's account of essences for abstract objects for all objects: A property F is essential to an object just in case it encodes that property. Like Zalta, we accept that if an object encodes a property, it encodes that property in every world in which it exists. We add an additional axiom to the theory: If x encodes F, then in any world in which x is concrete, x exemplifies F. This axiom governs both possibly concrete objects and abstract objects, although the latter only trivially. Given that nothing can exemplify inconsistent properties, the axiom implies that possibly concrete objects never encode inconsistent properties. (Nothing said prohibits abstract objects, such as the round square, from encoding inconsistent properties, that is, properties that cannot be jointly exemplified.)

It is part of our conception of what Sherlock Holmes is that he is a detective. Object theory makes sense of this by having Sherlock Holmes encode that property. But it is not part of our conception of Sherlock Holmes that he is a member of his singleton set. He fails to encode that property. (But Sherlock Holmes does exemplify this property, and does so as a matter of necessity!) But we make similar remarks about Socrates. It is part of our conception of what Socrates is that he is a human being, but not that he is a member of his singleton set. A uniform way of making sense of these remarks is that Socrates encodes humanity but not being a member of the singleton of Socrates.

Although I have just mentioned our conceptions of objects, I am not suggesting that which objects encode which properties is a consequence of what concepts we happen to have . This is not consonant with the background metaphysics in which there is a domain of abstracta whose existence and essence is independent of us. Rather, in the case of abstracta, because there are so many of them – roughly, for any set of encodable properties, there is an abstract object that encodes all and only those properties – our conceptions are bound to latch on to something. With respect to abstracta, our conceptions are excellent guides to essences: Because there are so many of them, our conceptions of an object are virtually guaranteed to match an object so conceived. With respect to actually concrete things, perhaps not. We have no a priori guarantee that a given conception perfectly tracks the essence of a concrete thing. But we know this. We know that it is much harder to discern the essence of Socrates than the essence of Sherlock Holmes.

The theory is remarkably simple, and as far as I can see free of counterexamples. One possible concern is whether Zalta's (2006) original theory correctly identified the essence of abstract objects; if it did not, the theory proposed here is in trouble too, since it delivers the same verdicts for abstract objects as Zalta's theory. So, consider Sherlock Holmes. One might think that Sherlock Holmes essentially depends on Arthur Conan Doyle. How do we capture this dependence if Sherlock Holmes encodes being a detective but doesn't encode any way of being related to Arthur Conan Doyle? It is not clear we need to. In Zalta's original theory, there is an entity that encodes all and only the properties Sherlock Holmes is depicted as having in the stories. But there is also an entity that encodes all these properties plus further properties that account for its being related to Arthur Conan Doyle. (Perhaps among these properties are being first thought of by Arthur Conan Doyle, or first written about by Arthur Conan Doyle, and so on.) The former entity is not essentially related to Arthur Conan Doyle, but the latter is. We can let our intuitions about essences assist us in deciding which entity is the referent of "Sherlock Holmes."

In what respect is this theory of essence that I have proposed reductive? If Fine says that a property is essential to x, the theory we are considering translates this as saying that x encodes the property. Rather than provide a reductive account of the phenomena, one might worry that the theory in question merely relabels it. I am not unduly concerned: What matters is that we have two ways of having a property instead of three. Whether to call the second way of having a property "encoding" or "inclusion in the essence of a thing" is of little importance.

Let us turn now to three objections to nonexistents.

1.5 Denials of Nonexistents

We've seen several reasons for accepting nonexistent objects in our metaphysics. We'll now look at several reasons against so-doing.

1.5.1 Thomasson on created fictional objects

We'll consider here Amie Thomasson's (1999) theory of created fictional objects. Although Thomasson's official position is neutral on whether fictional objects, such as Sherlock Holmes, exist, and whether, in general, existence and quantification coincide, there is a version of Thomasson's view that denies the former and affirms the latter. On this view, Sherlock Holmes exists, contrary to the Meinongian position. But Sherlock Holmes does not have the properties the stories attribute to him: He is not a detective or a user of cocaine. But he does have the property of being depicted as a detective and the property of being depicted as a user of cocaine. In general, for any property P such that the canonical stories about Holmes depict him as having P, Holmes has the property of being depicted as having P.

Holmes exists, but he is not the same kind of thing as you and I. Instead, Holmes is a contingently existing abstract object who owes his existence to the creative activities of the author of his stories.

Suppose that the sole reason to endorse Meinongianism is its treatment of fictional discourses, namely that it makes sense of how talks about Santa Claus and Spider-Man have distinctive subject matters. (As already noted, Meinong himself viewed this as but one of many reasons to endorse his view.) Thomasson's view seems to do at least as good as Meinongianism on this score, however. And it might even do better: On standard versions of Meinongianism, what objects there are is a matter of necessity, rather than contingency. So, there is a possible world in which, for example, Spider-Man is an object but Stan Lee does not exist to "create" him. In general, given Meinongianism, it is hard to see why it is apt to say that in the actual world Stan Lee *created* Spider-Man; instead, it seems that Stan Lee is better described as discovering him.[38] This is a counterintuitive consequence of standard Meinongianism, but it is not a consequence of Thomasson's view. So, if the sole reason to endorse Meinongianism is its treatment of fictional discourse, it seems that one has a better reason to endorse Thomasson's view instead.

There is, however, a wrinkle worth considering. If Stan Lee is the creator, rather than the discoverer, of Spider-Man, we should expect that the only possible worlds in which Spider-Man exists are worlds in which Stan Lee exists and engages in the relevant creative activities. And Thomasson's view implies just this. But similarly, we should expect that Spider-Man is created at a certain moment in time, and is not located at any time prior to this. So, for example, Spider-Man did not exist during the nineteenth century, but did exist during the 1970s, and continues to exist now. So, Spider-Man is an entity located in time.

It is intuitive that Spider-Man is located in time. But it is pretty weird if he is located in space as well. If he is located, where is he located? Is he located wherever the depictions of him are located? Perhaps this is the most credible answer if he is located at all. Might he be without location in space? Not if standard treatments space and time in relativistic physics are correct. In relativistic physics, there is no clean division between space and time, but rather there

---

[38] Compare with Thomasson (1999: 14–17).

is one arena: space-time. In special relativity, for one thing to be simultaneous with another relative to a reference frame is just for them to occupy regions of space-time that are part of the same three-dimensional hyperplane determined by that reference frame. But anything on such a hyperplane is as close to spatially located as anything actually is: Such hyperplanes are in effect the totality of space at a time (relative a frame). So, given special relativity (and relativistic physics more general), loosely speaking, Spider-Man is in time if and only if Spider-Man is in space, and strictly speaking, Spider-Man is either in space-time or not in space-time. There is no room for a merely temporally located Spider-Man in a relativistic world like ours. I will leave the reader to judge whether it is an acceptable consequence of Thomasson's view that Spider-Man is in space as much as he is in time.

1.5.2 Van Inwagen on Meinong

Van Inwagen's (1998) article "Meta-Ontology" gave a name to a discipline he helped shepherd into being – though given the doctrines defended therein, he would not be happy with the idea that anything can be shepherded *into* being. Here, we discuss one of van Inwagen's arguments against Meinongianism.

There is an account of Meinong's late-in-life renunciation of nonexistent objects. Because Meinong was blind near the end of his life, he wrote his correspondence with a typewriter rather than with a pen, and so it is comparatively easy to read and transcribe his letters. Meinong's correspondence with other philosophers can be read with profit. There is a letter that Meinong wrote to Russell shortly before Meinong passed away, in which Meinong admits that Russell not only refuted the positing of nonexistent objects but also provided convincing arguments against existent yet merely possible objects as well. Of course, this letter to Russell does not exist.[39]

Probably, when you got to previous sentence, you felt deceived! Van Inwagen would claim that you are right to feel deceived, because you were deceived – and that's because to say that there is such a letter and to say that the letter exists is fundamentally to say the same thing. In short, the indignation you feel about this story is the basis of an argument against Meinongianism.[40] You were deceived; you were deceived because you took Meinong's letter to exist when I told you that there was such a letter; and you did this because you recognize

---

[39] Compare with the fictional story that van Inwagen (1998: 236) tells about his conversation with his friend Wyman.

[40] Van Inwagen (1998: 236) writes that his "refusal to recognize a distinction between existence and being is simply my indignation, recollected in tranquility and generalized."

that there is no metaphysical difference between saying that there is something and saying that this something exists.

However, there are other explanations for why you were right to feel deceived that are compatible with Meinongianism. You reasonably took me to be talking about only objects that exist when I recounted the above story. We know that people usually don't intend to talk about absolutely everything when they use the words "everything" or "all." Instead, they typically have in mind only a narrower domain of things, specifically, those that are relevant to the ongoing conversation. The philosopher's stock example here is a stock example because it nicely illustrates this point: we are at a party, and you ask where the beer is, and I reply, "All the beer is in the fridge"; my reply is true even though there is much that is beer that is not in the fridge, such as the beer that is in Milwaukee and the beer that is in Germany. These other beers are not relevant to our conversation, and so we rightfully neglect them. Because they are rightfully neglected, they are not in the domain of the quantifier "all" when it is used in this context; "all" has been contextually restricted. But the same can be said of "there is," "some," "at least one": In a context in which the domain of "all" is restricted, the domain of these expressions is restricted as well; and this is because, in given context, the domain of one of these quantificational expressions is the domain of all the others.

In many ordinary contexts, we do not quantify over nonexistent objects, even if in some ordinary contexts we seem to. (In a context in which we are explicitly talking about fiction and characters in fictions, we at least seem to quantify over nonexistents.) Admittedly, you are reading a philosophy book, and so it is hard to say what context you were in when you read the story of Meinong's correspondence presented above. But that you felt deceived is good evidence that you at least took yourself to be in a context in which only existent objects were quantified over. The upshot is that the indignation you felt about the story I opened this section with doesn't provide much evidence against Meinongianism.

There might be a second reason why you were deceived – I wrote that there was a letter written by Meinong. But if there is a distinction between exemplifying and encoding a property, as some versions of Meinongianism claim, then you plausibly took me to be saying that there is an object that *exemplifies* the property of being a letter from Meinong to Russell. But if this letter doesn't exist, and if being a letter is a property that a nonexistent thing can merely encode rather than exemplify, then I plausibly mislead you into thinking that this object exemplified being a letter.

But let's focus on the first reason. If we are in a context in which nonexistent are not merely irrelevant to the conversation but also introducing them would thwart the purpose of that conversation, then plausibly we are in a context in which they are not within the domain of quantification. Perhaps even this is the context in which the philosopher who denies Meinongianism is apt to find himself in: and so perhaps this philosopher is unwittingly restricting the quantifier when he claims that there are no things that do not exist. If this is so, what the philosopher says is true – but what is said is nonetheless consistent with Meinongianism. This is a charitable way in which the Meinongian can interpret this philosopher. We will explore similar ideas in the next section.

1.5.3 Lewis on Noneism and Allism

Consider a list of dubious metaphysical entities: propositions, properties, possible worlds, sets, inconsistent objects, and beyond. The noneist thinks that none of these things exist; the allist things that all of them do. Interim positions are possible.

Let *Anti-Meinongianism* be the thesis that, necessarily, everything exists. Lewis (1990) endorses anti-Meinongianism, and is attracted to an interim position on what exists. Lewis raises the following question: How should the anti-Meinongian understand the Meinongian when he says that there are things that do not exist? The Meinongian makes a distinction that the anti-Meinongian does not, and Lewis portrays it as a distinction between two kinds of "existential" quantification, *loaded* and *unloaded*, which the Meinongian takes to correspond to *existence* and *being an object*. A related question is whether the anti-Meinongian should interpret the Meinongian as a noneist or an allist; this question is not settled by the Meinongian claiming to be a noneist while also claiming that each of things in the above list is among what there is, that is, is an object.

In the next section, we will confront similar issues about how from the perspective of one theory apparently competing theories should be interpreted. On the assumption that we are anti-Meinongians, we do not distinguish between quantification and existence. So, there are two prima facie viable interpretations of the Meinongian's vocabulary. Either the Meinongian's inner quantifier means the same thing as our quantifier or the Meinongian's outer quantifier means the same thing as our quantifier.

Let's consider the first interpretation: The inner quantifier means the same thing as our quantifier. Although this interpretation is credible – and it makes sense of how a Meinongian could assert noneism – on the whole, Lewis (1990: 26–28) thinks we should set it aside. On this interpretation, the Meinongian's outer quantifier should be understood as a simulation of a quantifier, one that might be equivalent to a complex expression in our language. Lewis's idea is that one simulates quantification when they use a quantificational expression in the scope of a sentential operator. An only child who does not believe in possible objects might still assert "possibly, I have a brother," and by doing this doesn't commit herself to a merely possible object.

Similarly, when the Meinongian asserts, "there are Greek gods," we might interpret them as meaning something like "According to Greek Mythology, there are Greek gods." However, the Meinongian also says things like "There are two gods of thunder, one of whom is Norse, and one of whom is Greek." And it is not true that, according to Greek mythology, there are two Gods of thunder, one of whom is Norse, and the other is Greek – and it is not true according to Norse mythology either. Is it true according to the conjunction of both mythologies? I'm honestly not sure, but maybe? On the other hand, the conjunction of two different mythologies seems to license massive contradictions, since each mythology tells a different, and incompatible, story of how the world was created, and so on – and who knows what is true according to an explicitly inconsistent story? Perhaps it is better to appeal to a more capacious expression, such as "According to the fiction that there are fictional objects, …." Regardless, Lewis (1990: 28) thinks that there is little textual evidence that this simulation of quantification is what the Meinongian has in mind.

Instead, Lewis (1990: 29) thinks that the anti-Meinongian should interpret the Meinongian's outer quantifier as corresponding to what the anti-Meinogian means by "there is" and "exists." So understood, the Meinongian who affirms all the problematic entities is an allist rather than a noneist – from the anti-Meinongian's perspective, the Meinongian asserts the existence of impossible worlds, inconsistent objects, and so on. This way of construing Meinongianism also has implication for how the debate between Meinongianism and anti-Meinongianism should be construed. From the perspective of the anti-Meinongian, the Meinongian falsely claims that there are/there exists entities with such and such features. From the perspective of the Meinongian, the anti-Meinongian is blind – she doesn't see that there is an interesting concept of existence that is both more restrictive than being in the domain of the outer quantifier and does not decide the substantive metaphysical question about what exists. Lewis (1990: 30), following D. C. Williams (1962), thinks that such a concept should be "dispensed with."

Let's pause here for a moment. Here are some things that Lewis does "see" – or, at least, here are some claims that Lewis endorses. First, classes of entities can be more or less *natural* in the sense of "carving at the joints," and at one end of the spectrum are the perfectly natural classes of things.[41] Perhaps the class of

---

[41] On natural properties, see Lewis (1986: section 1.5).

all the electrons is an example of a perfectly natural class, and the class of things I thought of yesterday is a good example of a much less than perfectly natural class. Let us provisionally assume that the class of objects that have spatiotemporal features is a highly natural class. Second, quantificational expressions, for example, "some," "most," "all," can be either explicitly or tacitly restricted, and when we do so, we can express truths. Recall the hackneyed example used earlier: "all the beer is in the fridge," which can be used to say something true even though there is a lot of beer not in the fridge. Consider now an explicit restriction of the outer quantifier to the natural class of things that have spatiotemporal properties. Isn't this explicitly restricted outer quantifier just the Meinongian's inner quantifier? And if it is, why does Lewis think that he can't "see" it?

However, on some versions of Meinongianism, nonexistent objects have spatiotemporal features. If the golden mountain is a mountain, then it must also be bigger than a hill, and being bigger than a hill is a spatiotemporal feature. More worrisome for this proposal is that the Meinongian's inner quantifier is not supposed to be *definitionally* equivalent to the outer quantifier conjoined with an explicitly restricting predicate, because if it were, the question about which things *exist*, that is, lie within the domain of the inner quantifier, would be trivial to answer. Instead, the Meinongia's inner quantifier is supposed to be *semantically primitive*, that is, an expression incapable of an explicit definition, just as the Meinongian's outer quantifier is supposed to be.[42] What Lewis does not see is how there could be a second semantically primitive (existential/particular) quantifier that is as important to metaphysics as the outer quantifier.

2 Are Ontological Debates Nonsubstantive?

2.1 Introduction

Metaphysicians by and large are earnest and serious. They conceptualize the task of metaphysics as the discovering of substantive truths about reality by way of philosophical investigation. Although a metaphysician might theorize about thought and language, or other ways of representing, they do so only in the service of theorizing about what that thought and language represents.[43] The

---

[42] The idea of a semantically primitive quantifier is prominent in the work of Eli Hirsch, which will be discussed in much detail in the next section. As Hirsch (2005: 76) puts it, "It seems perfectly intelligible to suppose that there can also be semantically restricted quantifiers, that is, quantifiers that, because of the semantic rules implicit in a language, are restricted in their range in certain specific ways. If the quantifiers in a language are semantically restricted, they are always limited in their range, regardless of the conversational context."

[43] The late and great Delia Graff Fara put it this way in the autobiographical remark that accompanied her photo in Pyke (2011): "By doing philosophy we can discover eternal and mind-independent truths about the "real" nature of the world by investigating our own conceptions of

metaphysician is interested in words like "freedom," "existence," "parthood," or our concepts of freedom, existence, or parthood, only insofar as examining them will shed light on freedom, existence, and parthood. We can imagine a project of trying to describe what our ordinary conceptions of freedom, existence, or parthood are, and such a project would be of value; Strawson (1964) calls this sort of project "descriptive metaphysics." But most metaphysicians do not construe what they are doing as merely descriptive metaphysics, which if done well produces merely a body of definitional or conceptual truths, rather than substantive truths about reality. This conception of the aims of metaphysics stretches at least as far back as Kant, who held that metaphysics as a science is possible only if it contains foundational synthetic a priori truths.[44]

This is especially true of ontologists. Perhaps most of metaphysics can be reconceptualized as descriptive metaphysics without a loss of its sense of importance. But can ontology be reconceptualized as descriptive ontology without loss?

Consider the special composition question: "under which conditions do some things compose a further thing?"[45] Putative answers include *universalism*, which is the view any things that have no parts in common compose a whole, *nihilism*, which is the view that many things never compose a further thing, *stuck togetherism*, which is the view that many things compose a thing when those things are sufficiently stuck together, and *organicism*, which is the view that many things compose a thing when the activity of those things constitutes a life.[46] For our purposes, having these four answers on the table suffices.

The debate between these four is an ontological debate, and judging by the quantity of attention it has received, it seems to be a substantive debate as well. But maybe this appearance is misleading. In what follows, we will first examine some metaontological positions that hold that this debate is not substantive. The first position, inspired by recent work by Eli Hirsch, is that the debate about composition is a merely verbal debate. The second position, also inspired by Eli Hirsch, is more subtle, but suffice it for now to say that it doesn't require the claim that the debates are merely verbal in the sense delineated by the first position. After examining these views and some responses to them, we will consider the metaontological position of Amie Thomasson, according to which

---

it, and by subjecting our most commonly or firmly held beliefs to what would otherwise be perversely strict scrutiny."

[44] See Kant's *Critique of Pure Reason* B17-B19 (1999: 145–146).
[45] See van Inwagen (1990) for an explanation of, and an attempt to answer, the special composition question, as well as for discussions of competing answers to it.
[46] Organicism is van Inwagen's preferred answer.

the debate about composition is "easily answered." And in Section 2.7, we will discuss the status of ontological pluralism and how it relates to these debates.

2.2 Hirsch and Quantifier Variantism

Imagine possible communities of human beings much like us except they take the answer to the special composition question to be obvious. Suppose the members of each of these communities speak languages that look and sound much like English – whether they speak English or the same language as each other will be explored more later in this section. One community thinks that universalism is obviously true, another thinks that nihilism is true, and so on. For them, the answer to the special composition question is as obvious as it is that bachelors are unmarried and that $7 + 5 = 12$. From our perspective, such a community is clearly possible even if we doubt it could be actual. For what would ground this consensus? Are the community members in a cult or obstinately dogmatic? Set the question about the ground of consensus aside for a moment – we will return to it.

Suppose members of one community come into contact with another. Suppose, for example, that members of the community that thinks that nihilism is obvious (henceforth: "the nihilist community") make contact with members of the community that thinks that universalism is obvious (henceforth: "the universalist community."). Initially, they are pleased at how much they agree on – they have the same mathematics, for example. But they are stunned when they learn the vast apparent differences between them with respect to composition – stunned enough that they wonder whether they are in fact speaking different languages rather than speaking the same language but disagreeing about obvious truths. After all, it is not very charitable to interpret your conversational partner as though he or she were making an obvious mistake if there are alternative interpretations of what he or she means available. And so members of these communities begin to look for alternative interpretations.

Pretend that you belong to the universalist community. When you say that there is something made of the xs, the members of the nihilist community seemingly say that there are only the xs. But you notice that whenever members of the nihilist community make a sentence that sounds like it uses a quantifier, what they say is necessarily equivalent to a sentence that does use a restricted quantifier whose domain contains only things without parts. And now you have a way of charitably interpreting your nihilist friends. They have an expression that functions like a quantifier, but it is *semantically primitive* (in the sense mentioned in the previous section). It's ok if you can't grasp its meaning in the way that people who grow up in that community can – it's enough that you now understand the truth conditions of sentences in which that expression appears. In this respect, your situation is better than the situation of Lewis with respect to the Meinongian: you can understand what is in effect the nihilist's "inner quantifier" because you can produce sentences necessarily equivalent to sentences in which it appears, whereas Lewis (allegedly) could not do that with respect to the Meinongian's inner quantifier.

Now pretend that you belong to the nihilist community, and that you are trying to understand the universalist community. They seem like crazy Meinongians to you – by your lights, they seem to be quantifying over what there isn't. But you recall from Lewis (1990) that there is a way to *simulate* quantification by placing prefixing an operator in front of a quantifier. When the Meinongian says something that sounds like "Most supervillains are more interesting than the heroes that are their archenemies," you understand them as saying something that is equivalent to "according to the fiction that there are fictional characters, most supervillains are more interesting than the heroes that are their archenemies." Perhaps that is what people in the universalist community are doing: they are doing something like simulating quantification. After much communication with them, your hypothesis bears fruit. There is a fiction – an absurd fiction, of course – that composition occurs whenever there are some things. And corresponding to this fiction is an operator, "according to the fiction of universal composition."[47] What you discover is this: Whenever the universalist uses a sentence that seemingly contains a quantifier, it is always necessarily equivalent to a sentence in your language that contains this operator followed by a genuine quantifier. For example, when the universalist says something that sounds like "there are tables," what they say is necessarily equivalent to the claim that you express by saying, "According to the fiction of universal composition, there are tables."

Now let's take a step back. Each community has a way of interpreting the other community so that the other community expresses reasonably believed truths rather than obvious falsehoods. Given this fact, it seems that members of either community have no reason to think that they genuinely disagree with the members of the other community, at least not about matters of ontology. There might be a disagreement about which language is a more convenient language to speak, though this disagreement might be pressing only once members of different communities have romantic entanglements with each other that result in children who must be raised and decisions about how to raise them.

Moreover, now each community can consider a hypothesis for why the other community finds what they say to be obviously true.[48] An expression is

---

[47] Compare with Rosen and Dorr (2002).   [48] Compare with Hirsch (2002b).

semantically primitive if and only if there is no complex expression within the language in which it appears that is equivalent in meaning to the original expression. But an expression can be semantically primitive and still yield conceptual truths. (For example, that red is a color.) The simplest conceptual truths stateable using semantically primitive expressions tend to be obviously true. Each community has an expression that functions like an existential quantifier in that the expression licenses the characteristic inference rules that govern that quantifier, namely existential instantiation and existential generalization, and similarly each community has an expression that functions like a universal quantifier. Moreover, each community's quantification-like expression yields a conceptual truth. When someone in the universalist community says something that sounds like "composition always occurs," what they express is a conceptual truth, and when someone in the nihilist community says something that sounds like "composition never occurs," what they say expresses a conceptual truth – and these conceptual truths are *compatible* with each other. (This is why there is no genuine ontological disagreement over whether composition occurs between the two communities.) These conceptual truths are expressed by easy-to-understand (if you belong to the relevant community) sentences, and so are easy to know as well – and this is why there is so much widespread agreement among members of a given community. For each community, there is something that sounds like the special composition question, and its answer is trivial and obvious. Given this, it seems that each of these languages is as good for describing reality as any of the others.

But what does this have to do with us? We don't belong to any of these communities, and the answer to when composition occurs is not obvious. And whatever that answer is, it doesn't seem to be a conceptual truth. But think now about how members of any of those communities will try to interpret us! Some of us believe in universalism; some of us believe in nihilism; some of us believe in organicism; and some of us believe in sufficiently stuck-togetherism. Each of these positions corresponds to a possible language in which sentences that sound like expressions of these positions express conceptual truths.[49] From their perspective, a plausible hypothesis is that it is unsettled or indeterminate which language we are using. And because it is unsettled, there is no fact of the matter about which of these positions is true – and no fact of the matter about which of these positions is a conceptual truth.

On the hypothesis that it is indeterminate which of these languages we speak, there is no *substantive* question about when composition occurs. Here is an analogy to consider. Consider the word "rich." How much money must

---

[49] Compare with Hirsch (2005).

someone have in order to be rich? It's indeterminate how much: There is no precise monetary amount necessary and sufficient for being rich because we never settled what that amount is.[50] But we could have settled this, and there are other languages that are exactly like English except that in them "bald" corresponds to a precise cutoff point; the languages differ from each other in where this cutoff point is drawn. In each of these languages, having fewer than some n number of hairs is necessary and sufficient for "bald" to apply, and in each of these languages, this is a conceptual truth. So, although it is indeterminate in our language which n corresponds to being bald, it is still a conceptual truth that there is some n such that having fewer than n hairs is necessary and sufficient for being bald. Similarly, although it is indeterminate which language we speak, it is determinate that on each language the answer to what sounds like the special composition question is a conceptual truth, whatever that answer might be.

Members of these other communities have a good reason to accept this hypothesis about us. Do we? Here is one reason for us to be cautious. Consider a language L that is a lot like English and that contains a sentence S that expresses a conceptual truth in L. Suppose that what S expresses in L is necessarily equivalent to what is expressed by a sentence E in English. It doesn't follow from this that E expresses a conceptual truth, or that the question of whether E is true is non-substantive. Imagine a community much like ours except that children are taught at an early age that the word "water" just means "substance consisting of H_2O molecules." In this language, the sentence "water is the substance consisting of H_2O molecules" expresses a conceptual truth, and the truth that it expresses is necessarily equivalent to the truth that we express when we say that water is the substance consisting of H_2O molecules. What we express is *not* a conceptual truth, but rather a synthetic empirical claim, albeit one that is necessarily true. It is a substantive claim because facts about the chemical makeup of water are not built into the semantics of "water" in English.[51] And it might be that in a similar way facts about the metaphysical constitution of reality are not built in the meaning of quantifier expressions – and so statements about what there is are substantive claims rather than assertions of conceptual truths.

If principles about when composition occurs, or other apparently basic ontological truths, are not baked into the semantics of quantifier expressions, what is? A plausible answer is the inferential principle governing those expressions.[52] So, for example, it is part of the meaning "something" that it follows from the claim that Charlie is a dog that something is a dog, and it is part

---

[50] Compare with Lewis (1986: 212).   [51] See Kripke (1981: lecture III).
[52] See Warren (2015: 241–242).

of the meaning "everything" that this inference is valid: if everything is finite, and Kris is among what there is, then Kris is finite. Is this it? That is, is merely obeying the characteristic inferential rules governing "something" necessary and sufficient for an expression to have the same meaning as our word "something"? If so, then our actual meaning for this expression is importantly different from the other putative alternative meanings for it; perhaps the differences are significant enough that we should not think of them as genuine alternative meanings. A related question is whether obeying these characteristic inference rules is necessary and sufficient for an expression to have the same meaning as "something" in our language. If it is, then these alleged alternative meanings for "something" do not exist, and quantifier variance is not possible![53]

In what follows, I will assume that the answer to this related question is "no," and so quantifier variance is not immediately ruled out. Given this answer, there is a further interesting question about why the quantifier-like expressions can be used to express *conceptual* truths about, speaking very loosely, what there is, while our expression cannot be so used. Can we imagine different languages that contain quantifier-like expressions such that speakers of those languages associate with those expressions concepts that are analogous to our concept of a domain of quantification, but for which it is not conceptually true what is included in this conception of a domain of quantification? That is, can we envision an alternative language to English in which the sentence in that language that sounds like "whenever there are some xs, there is a y composed of those xs" expresses a truth that is a substantive rather than conceptual truth, and similarly for the other alternative languages we are considering?

Thus far, I have focused on the contrast between conceptual truths and nonconceptual truths, and have labeled the latter "substantive." The idea was to explore the thought that not much is really at stake in putative ontological debates if the answers to the corresponding ontological questions are always either conceptually true or conceptually false or conceptually indeterminate. And, as already noted, this way of considering the question of substantivity was driven by the Kantian idea that, in general, metaphysics aims to discover nonconceptual truths, and is thus bankrupt as an enterprise if it cannot succeed in this aim. But perhaps there is a different way of demarcating the substantive from the nonsubstantive that doesn't closely track the distinction between conceptual and nonconceptual truths. Perhaps the mere fact that there are possible alternative languages of the sort that we have envisioned in which sentences that sound like "composition always occurs" or "composition never occurs" express truths is

---

[53] That satisfying the inferential role of the existential quantifier is necessary and sufficient for meaning what we mean by "something" is suggested (but not defended) by Eklund (2021).

sufficient to make the debate over composition nonsubstantive – even if in those languages the sentences express truths that are not conceptual truths. Let's explore this furthermore.

The *semantic value* of an expression is whatever object directly partially grounds the truth conditions of sentences in which that expression occurs. Plausibly, any entity can be the semantic value of a name; I am the semantic value of the name "Kris." And, plausibly, the semantic values of predicates are properties. What about quantifiers? A natural answer, which I will assume in what follows, is that the semantic values of quantifiers are higher-order relations, that is, relations that relate properties.[54] Consider the sentence "some dogs are red." On the natural answer, the semantic value of "some" is a relation that relates the property of being a dog and the property of being red if and only if at least one dog is red.

The binary relation that is the semantic value of "some" is conditionally reflexive in this sense: If property F bears this relation to property G, property F bears this relation itself. (This is because the fact that some F is F follows from the fact that some F is G.) It is also symmetric. (This is because the fact that some G is F follows from the fact that some F is G.) But it is not transitive. (It does not follow that some F is H from the fact that F is G and some G is H.) In general, binary relations are exemplified by two things (or one thing twice over), and for any binary relation, there is a set of ordered pairs such that the first element of a pair bears that relation to the second element of that pair; such a set is *the extension* of that relation. Here is a hypothesis: The semantic values of the words that sound "something" in these alternative languages we are considering also have higher-order binary relations that are conditionally reflexive and symmetric but otherwise differ with respect to their extensions. Given this hypothesis, the alternative languages contain expressions that are quantifier expressions, and I will call these possible semantic values "alternative quantifier values."

In virtue of what is something the semantic value of an expression? This is a *metasemantic* question, and one of direct relevance to metaontology. An initial first answer is facts about how that expression is used. Among other things, expressions are used to assert propositions that speakers take to be true. For any expression in a given language, there is a set of sentences that speakers of that language are disposed to sincerely assert. An *interpretation* of a set of sentences is an assignment of semantic values to the expressions appearing in that sentence. An interpretation of a set of sentences is *charitable* to the extent that the sentences in that set are true given that interpretation. Our initial first answer says that an

---

[54] See Westerståhl (2011) for a discussion of the semantic values of quantifiers.

expression E has semantic value S in virtue of the fact that the most charitable interpretation of the set of sentences that contain E that speakers are disposed to assert is one which E is assigned the semantic value S.[55]

This initial first answer needs revising, and we will come that to soon enough, but for now observe that this metasemantic theory doesn't appeal to a distinction between conceptual and nonconceptual truths – all sentences in a set to be interpreted count equally when it comes to charity, as construed above. We could have a more complicated theory in which there is stratification: some sentences, perhaps those speakers that of the community regard as conceptual truths, count for more than others when determining how charitable an interpretation of them is.[56] But we won't develop this more complicated theory here, since our current goal is to see whether there is a way of making the debate over composition nonsubstantive without appealing to the idea of conceptual truth. We will, however, consider a second way of stratifying sentences that appeal to the average level of confidence speakers have when asserting sentences. In general, on average, speakers are disposed to very confidently assert "the sun will rise tomorrow" and "2 + 3 = 5," and are disposed to fairly confidently assert "composition sometimes occurs."

Recall that speakers of these alternative languages are very confident in their seemingly ontological assertions – unlike speakers of our languages! And so on the second way of measuring the charity of interpretation, we heavily favor an assignment of a quantifier value to a quantifier expression that makes those confident assertions come out true. These assertions are confidently made, but this does not make them conceptual truths; we confidently assert "the sun will rise tomorrow," but this sentence does not express a conceptual truth.

To sum up where we are so far, there are possibly alternative languages that contain quantifier expressions that sound and function like our expression "some," and that have different semantic values than the value of "some," and these different semantic values have a different extension than extension of the semantic value of "some." In one of these languages, a sentence that sounds like "composition always occurs" expresses a truth; in another language, a sentence that sounds like "composition never occurs" expresses a truth. On the other hand, it is not clear whether when we say, "composition always occurs," what we say is true, or false, or indeterminate. We have not yet captured the idea though that the question of when composition occurs is nonsubstantive. But we just need one extra ingredient to do so: the claim that, from a metaphysical

---

[55] Compare with Hirsch (2002a; 2002b). For worries about charity, see Balcerak-Jackson (2013) and Sider (2014).
[56] Compare with Sider (2011: 192–195).

perspective, each of these alternative quantifier values is as a good as each other and as good as the semantic value of our quantifier, and so there is no metaphysical respect in which one of these languages does a better job than any of the others when it comes to describing reality.

Is this extra ingredient true?

2.3 Sider on "Structure"

The distinction between properties that carve nature closer to the joints and those that do not is well-entrenched contemporary metaphysics, largely due to the work of David Lewis (1983, 1984, 1986). The distinction between properties that account for genuine and objective similarities between things is intuitive: dogs have something importantly in common with each other by virtue of being dogs, while dogs and cats do not have something importantly in common with each other by virtue of not being violins. But Lewis argued that this intuitive distinction does real philosophical work: Among other things, it is useful for characterizing supervenience, what makes a generalization a law of nature, what distinguishes intrinsic and extrinsic properties, and what makes a word refer to something. When a distinction is both intuitive and theoretically useful in a variety of contexts, it is reasonable to look for additional contexts in which it can be employed. This is what Sider (2009, 2011) does: Sider argues that we can "go beyond the predicate": not only do some predicates correspond to nature's joints, perhaps in virtue of referring to properties that carve at the joints, but so too do some quantifiers, and perhaps so too do other expressions, such as sentential operators and connectors.

That some quantifiers correspond more to joints than others is somewhat intuitive. Consider the difference between "some dog is red" and "exactly seven dogs or exactly 13 dogs or between 935 and 2036 dogs are red." Isn't the quantifier contained in the second sentence more gerrymandered or gruesome than the one in the first sentence? It wears its disjunctiveness on its face. Furthermore, consider that one reason for thinking that a predicate corresponds to a highly natural property is that this predicate (or one coreferential with it) appears in highly a successful theory. Similarly, though, Sider (2011: 188) argues that the existential quantifier appears in highly successful theories in physics, mathematics, logic, and so on. So insofar as appearing in successful theories is a good guide to corresponding to naturalness, there is a good case that the existential quantifier corresponds to a natural joint. Given that there are both intuitive and theoretical considerations that favor it, Sider's modest extension of Lewis's conception of naturalness is accordingly reasonable. Sider calls the view that the existential quantifier corresponds to a quantificational joint "ontological realism."

A possible response is that Sider's argument supports the claim that the existential quantifier appearing in physical theories and the existential quantifier appearing in mathematical theories correspond to quantificational joints. But does Sider's argument support the claim that these quantifiers are strictly the same? Maybe there are two quantificational joints.[57] Perhaps it does when supplemented with a claim about simplicity: the hypothesis that there is one, rather than two, quantificational joints is a simpler hypothesis, and that it provides a reason to believe it over its alternatives.

Sider (2009) endorses a view that has come to be called "reference magnetism." According to reference magnetism, one of the factors that determines whether an expression refers to (or has as its semantic value) a given entity is how natural that entity is both in absolute terms and relative to other candidate referents of the expression. The more natural a thing is, the more referential pull it possesses. A sufficient degree of naturalness can trump use so that the correct interpretation of what we say is one in which we say many falsehoods. Both the naturalness of candidate referents and the charitableness of an interpretation come in degrees, and no one knows how much naturalness it takes to trump a certain amount of charitableness. Broadly speaking, then, even given that there is a perfectly natural quantificational joint, there are two possibilities: It is sufficiently natural to trump charitableness and so it is the referent of the ordinary English expression "something," or it is not. In the former case, ontological disputes conducted in English are not merely verbal in Hirsch's sense; in the latter case, they might be, but if they are, there is a fallback option: Conduct the debates in an artificial language in which quantificational expressions are *stipulated* to refer to the quantificational joints. Sider calls this language "Ontologese." According to Sider, debates about "what there is" in Ontologese are substantive debates.

Ontologese contains expressions that function analogously to how quantifiers function. In a moment, I will want to ask some questions *in* (rather than *about*) Ontologese, so let me introduce a convention: When an English expression is followed by an "*," that expression's semantic value is that perfectly natural entity that is the closest candidate among all other perfectly natural entities for being the semantic value of the English expression. (If there is a tie for closeness here, let us stipulate that the English expression followed by the "*" fails to have a semantic value rather than ambiguously has more than one.) So, for example, "there is*" expresses the analogue of existential quantification of in Ontologese.

---

[57] This view would be a form of ontological pluralism, which will be discussed in Section 2.7.

Sider (2011) doesn't believe that there is* very much. His preferred ontology* is one in which there are* the fundamental entities that will be posited by our best physics, and perhaps in addition to those entities there are* sets, but not much else. I say this neither to praise nor to criticize this ontology*, but rather because it raises an interesting question about Sider's *ontology* (rather than his ontology*): Is it an ontology that contains *nonexistent objects*?

The answer to this question might depend on whether "there is" and "there is*" have the same semantic value. Let's assume that they do not, and that charity has trumped naturalness when it comes to determining the semantic value of "there is." Given this claim, although "there are tables" is true, "there are* tables" is not true. Recall that, in Section 1, in the context of discussing Aristotelian meta-ontologies, I considered the proposal that to exist is to belong to one of the Aristotelian categories. On my view, what would distinguish the Aristotelian categories from other ways of carving up the world into classes of entities is that the Aristotelian categories would correspond to genuine *ways* of being – where a way of being is a quantificational joint.[58] A prima facie reasonable generalization of this idea is that for x to exist is to have a way of being in this sense, that is, for there to be a possible quantifier whose semantic value is a quantificational joint and that quantifies over x. Here is why this generalization is reasonable: if being something – that is, being quantified over – is different from existing, then it seems that what matters when assessing whether a theory's ontology is *costly* is what the theory says exists. Similarly, though, if being something is different from being something*, then what matters when assessing whether a theory's ontology is costly is what the theory says about what there is*. Either there are two things relevant to the costliness of an ontology or what exists just is what there is*.

Given this reasonable generalization, and given that "there are tables" is true, "there are* tables" is not true, it follows that tables do not exist, even though there are tables. This consequence is a bit weird, and we will discuss in a moment about how to avoid it. But note also that, like the Meinongian views discussed in Section 1, the position that we are discussing distinguishes both an "inner" and "outer" quantifier, because whenever "there are* Fs" is true, "there are Fs" is true, but the converse is not always the case. On the Meinongian theories, the inner quantifier corresponds to that which exists.

In light of this discussion, perhaps we should reconsider the generalized idea that to exist is to have a way of being. "Exist," like "there is," is an expression of ordinary English. If charity trumps naturalness with respect to the latter, it is hard to see why it would not with respect to the former. An interpretation of

---

[58] This is defended in McDaniel (2017: chapter four).

"tables exist" that makes it false doesn't seem very charitable. If "exists" does not carve at the joints, then perhaps what exists and what is costly in ontology come apart. This is what Ross Cameron (2010) suggests: We are ontologically committed to what our best theories say exists* rather than what they say exists.

These remarks suggest that it is not necessary for an entity to exist that it has a way of being. Maybe it is not sufficient either! Recall that Meinong's official view seems to be one in which both the inner quantifier *and* the outer quantifier correspond to quantificational joints.[59] But then it follows from the generalized idea that if Meinong's official view is true, then absolutely everything exists – even the nonexistent round square!

It seems then that the generalized idea should be scrapped, despite its initial plausibility. Scrapping it, however, then leaves open a question that we would like answered, namely, what is existence?

Let's return to the discussion of ontological realism. One worry is that it generates hard questions about naturalness that might seem to be pseudo questions.[60] There is the existential quantifier and the universal quantifier. It is hard to see why one of them would be more natural than the other. But if they are equally natural, and both correspond to a quantificational joint, then it seems that there is kind of metaphysical redundancy: Why does the world have two joints here when every theoretical purpose served by positing just one of them? Perhaps redundancy is preferable to arbitrariness, but probably better not to have to choose.[61] That said, the same sort of problem already faced Lewis's original theory of naturalness. For example, every nonsymmetric relation has a converse. Some nonsymmetric relations might be highly natural. But if so, is the converse relation equally natural? For example, perhaps *is earlier than* is a highly natural relation; but if so, what should be said about its converse *is later than*?

Perhaps there are no perfectly natural nonsymmetric relations, and more generally, whenever there is apparently redundant perfectly natural properties or relations, none of the properties or relations are perfectly natural. This is an interesting hypothesis, but if true, it is hard to see how to defend it.[62] Moreover, the natural extension of this hypothesis is that whenever there are some features that are inter-definable with each other, then none of these features are perfectly

---

[59] More precisely two inner quantifiers, either disjoint or nested. I suggest this interpretation of Meinong in McDaniel (2017: 37–39).

[60] This is the worry Sider (2011: chapter 10) raises for his own view. One possibility worth considering is that we cannot know the logical structure of the world; this is defended by McSweeney (2019).

[61] See Sider (2011: 219).

[62] One possible way to defend it is to deny that there are any nonsymmetric relations period! See Dorr (2004) for a defense of this claim.

natural. This natural extension implies that ontological realism is false.[63] However, this fallback position would not be refuted: that there is a most natural meaning for the existential quantifier, even if it is not a perfectly natural meaning. Call this position *ontological near realism*.[64]

Ontological near realism might suffice to respond to Hirsch's challenge, provided that this most natural meaning is natural enough to trump charity to enough extent that it ends up being what is meant when ontological disputes are conducted. And even if it is not natural enough, one could still conduct disputes in the language of *Near Ontologese.*

Moreover, there is something like an inductive reason to take ontological near realism seriously. Let's consider our track record when it comes to discovering perfectly natural properties or relations. What actually is our success rate? We have learned that properties that we might have thought were good candidates for being perfectly natural properties or relations are not really: colors, shapes, simultaneity, among others, are not perfectly natural. We hypothesize that some of the properties currently postulated by what we regard as fundamental physics are perfectly natural properties – but I don't think we *know* this. It seems like it is really hard work to discover the perfectly natural properties and relations exemplified by concrete objects. Why think that we are doing better with respect to the perfectly natural properties and relations in logic? Even though, as Husserl and Frege persuasively argued, logic is not the study of how to reason properly, logic, including quantificational logic, was developed to be a tool to aid us in improving our reasoning. How lucky we are to hit on a perfectly natural quantificational feature so early on![65]

2.4 Amie Thomasson and Easy Ontology

Consider two arguments, unimaginably labeled "A1" and "A2."

A1: There are as many shoes in the room as there are feet in the room.

So, the number of shoes in the room is the same as the number of feet in the room.

A2: There are prime numbers between 2 and 9.

So, there are numbers.

---

[63] It would also imply that ontological pluralism is false.
[64] As we will see shortly, some versions of ontological pluralism imply ontological near realism even though they are incompatible with ontological realism.
[65] See again McSweeney (2019).

Here are some initial comments about these arguments. A1 is not formally valid, although it seems that the conclusion in some sense follows from its premise. Determining in what sense though is the primary task of this section. There are many contexts in which the premise of this argument would be taken as obviously true, but in each of these contexts, the truth expressed would be an empirical rather than a priori truth. A2, on the other hand, is formally valid. And there are many contexts in which its premise would be taken as obviously true, though in this case, the truth is a priori. However, some philosophers are notoriously skeptical about whether there are numbers. They seem to think it is not obvious whether the conclusions of these arguments are true. What's going on?

Let's focus for now on A1, and let's imagine some philosophers who think that, although it is a hard question whether there are numbers, there are in fact numbers. What is the sense in which the conclusion of A1 follows from its premise? Plausibly, on their view, the sense is this: It is an argument with a suppressed premise that when made explicit yields a formally valid argument. That suppressed premise is this: Some things and some other things can be put in a one-to-one correspondence if and only if the number of the first things is identical with the number of the second things.

What is the epistemic status of this biconditional? Here we find division in their ranks. Some of these philosophers think that this biconditional is known by way of a special faculty of rational insight that can peer into the realm of abstract objects. This view does sound a bit akin to mysticism, especially since it is difficult to see what physical correlates to the faculty could realize it – unlike our various empirical perceptual faculties, for which there are well-developed scientific theories of how they work. Accordingly, these philosophers might be somewhat confident of the deliverances of this alleged faculty, but worries about whether this faculty actually exists prevent them from being too confident.

A second group of philosophers think that this biconditional is supported by its inclusion in a well-supported theory, such as the theory that there are numbers. What makes this theory well-supported is that it explains that data it is meant to explain in a fruitful, simple, and coherent way.[66] Do fruitfulness, simplicity, and coherence track truth? Not obviously invariably, especially when these theoretical virtues are appealed to metaphysical rather than empirical contexts. Are these philosophers making a leap of faith that they are? Or does the fact that theories that have these virtues are easier for us to formulate, believe, and apply itself provide a pragmatic reason to believe them?[67] These

---

[66] See Paul (2012) and Brenner (2023) for discussions of the appeal to theoretical virtues in metaphysics and science.

[67] Bricker (2006: 44) suggests that appeals to theoretical benefits do not provide reasons to believe the theory.

are hard questions. Whatever their answers might be, the difficulty of these questions suggests that the biconditional that is the implicit premise of A1 should be endorsed only tentatively.

All these philosophers agree that the question of whether this biconditional is true is a hard question. However, if it is a hard question whether this biconditional is true, it is also a hard question whether the conclusion of A2 is true.[68] And since A2 is a formally valid argument, this means that it is also a hard question whether the premise of A2 is true. But it seemed that there were plenty of contexts in which this premise is obviously true! How can a question be hard if there are contexts in which it is easily answered?

Maybe this question should lead us to rethink something. Amie Thomasson (2015) has argued that what we should rethink is the claim that it is a hard question whether the biconditional implicitly in play in A1 is true. On the contrary, this is an easy question: It is obviously true, because it is an obvious conceptual truth. Consider a second example illustrating this idea. It's obvious, to me anyways, that I have as many toes as I have fingers. And it is an obvious conceptual truth that I have as many toes as I have fingers if and only if the number of my toes is the same as the number of my fingers. (This conceptual truth is an instance of the more general conceptual truth mentioned earlier.) It follows from these two claims via an obviously valid inference that the number of my toes is the same as the number of my fingers. And it follows from this via an obviously valid argument that there are numbers. How then could the question of whether there are numbers be a hard question for me to answer? How obtuse would I have to be to not know the answer given all of this?

Maybe the question that I am trying to ask – the question that I think is a hard question – isn't really the question of whether there are numbers. Maybe it is the question of whether numbers are real; or maybe it's the question of whether a metaphysically fundamental quantifier would quantify over numbers.[69] But, as we will discuss later in this section, Thomasson thinks that these questions are pseudo-questions: There is no additional question of this sort to even ask, so there is no hard question in the neighborhood of the easily answered question.

Let's consider another ontological debate that, according to Thomasson, is easily settled: the debate over whether there are ordinary objects such as chairs and tables. As Thomasson notes (2007: 155–170; 2015: 129–130), compositional

---

[68] It might be that nonetheless arguments like A2 are more apt to succeed as easy ontological arguments than arguments like A1. For example, Felka (2016) argues that a sentence like "The number of moons of Mars is two" is not an identity sentence, and so doesn't by itself support an easy argument for numbers. Even if Felka is correct, the status of A2 as an easy argument for numbers is unaffected. I thank an anonymous referee for directing my attention to Felka's book.

[69] The Meinongian might think it is the former, while someone attracted to Sider's view might think it is the latter.

nihilists try to "save the appearances" by describing the conditions under which assertions that an ordinary object exists is well-founded even if strictly false; for example, the claim expressed by "a table exists" is well-founded if and only if there are some impartite entities arranged in a table-like configuration.[70] But, according to Thomasson, it is a trivial conceptual truth that whenever there are some impartite entities arranged in a table-like configuration, there is a table. And so the well-foundedness conditions for assertions about tables presented by the nihilist are really truth conditions for assertions about tables. On her view, nihilism is accordingly trivially (and obviously) false.

Let's pause for a moment. What does "some impartite entities are arranged in a table-like configuration" mean? And can this meaning be explained without assuming that there are tables? For example, "some impartite entities are arranged in a table-like configuration if and only if their collective shape is the shape of a paradigmatic table" presupposes that there are paradigmatic tables. Eliminativism is in serious trouble if the only accounts of the well-foundedness of ordinary table judgments presuppose the existence of tables! But in a similar way, it will be harder to show that it is trivially true that nihilism is false if the conceptual truths appealed to explicitly presuppose the existence of composite objects. Consider two different claims.

C1: If there are impartite entities arranged in a table-like configuration, then there is a table.

C2: If there are impartite entities arranged in a table-like configuration and they compose something, then there is a table.

If the only way to secure the conceptual truth of C1 is to unpack "table-like configuration" so that to be in a table-like configuration means, among other things, that composition has occurred, then the fact that C1 so understood is a conceptual truth doesn't show that it is trivial or obvious that nihilism is false. Similarly, if C2 is a conceptual truth, but C1 is not, we do not have an easy argument against nihilism, since it is compatible with nihilism that C2 is a conceptual truth. So, it seems that both eliminativism and Thomasson's view require definitions of expression like "table-like configuration" that do not explicitly assume that there are tables, or even that there are composite objects. Eliminativism is arguably refuted if such definitions are impossible; Thomasson's view would not be refuted, but would be unmotivated, at least as it applies to the debate over nihilism.

In general, for any kind of thing, Ks, such that it is a putatively easy question whether there are Ks, two conditions must be met. First, there must be a noncircular way to state claims of the form: if there is a K-favorable

---

[70] See also Bennett (2009).

circumstance, then there is a K.[71] Second, it must be obvious that there are K-favorable circumstances. (If it is an empirical claim that there are K-favorable circumstances, then it is an obviously true empirical claim.) Much attention has been focused on whether the first condition can be met; you got a taste of this debate in the previous paragraphs.[72] But note that, although the most ambitious version of Thomasson's position is one which *all* ontological debates are easily settled, this is not a version that Thomasson herself is committed to. Moreover, even if it turns out that there is no general way to show that all ontological questions are easily settled, a piecemeal version of Thomasson's view on which this ontological question (e.g., are there numbers?) is easily settled, and that ontological question (e.g., are there composite objects?) is easily settled, and this one, and so on, is still an interesting view that would challenge many *metaontological* approaches to these specific questions.

This is good to keep in mind, because there do seem to be some hard ontological questions even given the conceptual truth of a relevant conditional claim – they are hard because it is not obvious whether the antecedent is satisfied. For example, consider the hard ontological question about whether there is a God. Consider now two claims that are plausibly conceptual truths.

G1: If something is holy, then there is a God that makes it holy.

G2: If, necessarily, everyone is loved by someone, then there is a God.

G1 is perhaps more clearly a conceptual truth than G2, though one might worry that there is no way to explicitly unpack what it is to be holy without including the consequent of G1 is in the definition. But suppose that there is – still, it is not at all obvious that anything is holy! It doesn't seem that the question of whether something is holy is much easier to answer than the question of whether there is a God. Attend now to G2. I think that no explicit definition of the antecedent will spit out the consequent. But G2 might be a conceptual truth nonetheless, though the argument for why it has this status is a little indirect: It is part of the conception of God that God is all-loving, and so if there is a God, then, necessarily, God loves everyone. But it also seems that the *only* way in which the antecedent of G2 could be true is if there is a God; on no other metaphysics does this seem guaranteed.[73] However, it is also not at all obvious that the antecedent of G2 is true, and it seems that the reason to think that G2 is

---

[71] This claim is a logically weaker consequence of what Thomasson (2015: 86–87) defends, but it will suffice for our purposes here to focus on it.
[72] See, e.g., Raab (2020) for concerns about circularity.
[73] Save perhaps for the love-infused yet atheistic metaphysics of McTaggart (1927); see McDaniel (2009) for discussion.

a conceptual truth is also a reason to think we have no more evidence for the antecedent than we do for the consequent.

Consider next the following:

T: Whenever two things are simultaneous, there is a time at which they are both present.

T strikes me as just as much of a conceptual truth as Thomasson's examples. (This claim is consistent with none of them being conceptual truths.) So, is the question of whether there are times easy? Surprisingly not – but that's because although it might have *seemed* obvious that there are things that are simultaneous, whether this is the case is a thorny question in both physics and the philosophy thereof. Given standard interpretations of the special and general theories of relativity, there is no such relation as the relation of simultaneity. A Thomassonian ontologist of the nineteenth century might have thought that the question of whether there are times is trivially settled, but she would have been mistaken. We thought there were simultaneous happenings, but we learned otherwise. No two things are ever simultaneous full stops; at best, they stand in a three-place relation of relative simultaneity, assuming that such reference frames are even well defined. (They might not be.)

Can't this sort of thing happen elsewhere? What if we just have the wrong theory of the world? For example, our conception of an event seems to be a conception of a happening in time. So, this seems like a conceptual truth: Something is an event only if it occurs in time. But if there are no times, then it follows that there are no events either.[74]

Let's consider the following:

S: If two things are spatiotemporally related, then there is a region of space-time that contains them both.

I'm inclined to think that S is true, and considerations from relativity do not render its antecedent vacuous. But I see no case for thinking that S is a conceptual truth! Rather, it is a substantive claim that is the core of what is at issue between relationalists and substantivalists about spatiotemporal connections. Moreover, whether S is true won't be settled by appeal to physics alone – metaphysical considerations such as appeals to explanatory power, simplicity, and other theoretical virtues will play an important role as well.[75] Whether S is true is a hard ontological question.

---

[74] Thomasson (2015: 129–130) argues that it is an easy ontological question whether there are events – there are events.
[75] See, e.g., North (2018).

How damaging is the hardness of the question of whether S is true to the thesis that ontology is easy? Whether S is true will not be settled purely by a priori speculation – physics will play a large role here. But the extent to which considerations of physics, or of empirical science more generally, are relevant to answering ontological questions corresponds to a difference in degree rather than kind. Consider the special composition question. I don't think it's obvious that empirical scientific considerations are wholly irrelevant to answering this question, and here are two different strands of reasoning that suggest their relevance. First, it is initially plausible that composition occurs when some the putative parts stand in some sort of bonding relation. But physics, chemistry, and other empirical sciences can offer better accounts of what sort of bonding relations there are than would be given by an analysis of our inchoate concepts of bonding. Second, it is prima facie plausible that if there are natural (as opposed to non-gerrymandered/gruesome) properties at different levels of nature (e.g., the chemical level, the biological level, etc.), then there must be composite objects that "occupy" those different levels and that instantiate those natural properties. Empirical scientific considerations are relevant to assessing whether there are natural properties at these different levels. Given that empirical scientific considerations are relevant, but not by themselves decisive, to the positive case for composite objects, they might also be relevant to the negative case as well.

We've discussed whether the ontology of numbers is easy.[76] Is the ontology of other mathematical domains as easy? Let's consider the question of whether there are sets. If the ontology of sets is easy, then there is a conditional that is conceptually true, whose antecedent is obvious, and whose consequence is a claim about the existence of some set or sets. What is this conditional? This might have seemed like a conceptual truth at the turn of the twentieth century: Whenever there are some entities and some predicates, there is a set of all and only those entities that satisfy the predicate. But this alleged conceptual truth generates the paradoxical set of all nonself-membered entities, as Russell (1967) pointed out.[77] What about this: Whenever there are things that do not have members, there is a set that contains all and only those things? This is

---

[76] One thing we have not discussed but has some important parallels to the discussion of set theory below in this section is whether there are competing conceptual rules for the application of numerical vocabulary. This possibility is raised by Plebani (2018: 308), who also argues that this possibility raises an interesting challenge to Thommasson's metaontology. I thank an anonymous reviewer for directing me to this paper.

[77] We are now in the neighborhood of the so-called bad company objection, which in a nutshell is the worry that the methodology of easy ontology will license the existence of inconsistent or impossible objects. See Thomasson (2015: chapter 8) for a discussion and response to this argument.

a plausible claim but is it a conceptual truth? This claim implies that there can't be more individuals than any set could contain, which is also plausible, but it's not clearly a conceptual truth. Perhaps the axioms of set theory are collectively conceptual truths – but which version of set theory? There are many, apparently competing, set theories. If the axioms of one, and not more than one, of these theories are true, which of these are true seems to be a substantive question about sets rather than a trivial question answerable by attending to our concept of a set.

However, maybe the assumption that these different set theories are in competition is not true. Consider the idea that the criterion for existence in mathematics is logical consistency.[78] This idea fits nicely with the idea that mathematical ontology is easy. So, consider a principle that explicitly weds them.

Conex: If a set theory S is logically consistent, then there are entities that obey the axioms of S.

Perhaps Conex is a conceptual truth. If Conex is a conceptual truth, then perhaps each of these apparently competing set theories are also conceptual truths, but are not in competition because the same concept of set is not used by each of these theories.[79] Let's explore this furthermore.

Suppose that Conex is a conceptual truth. Consider a particular set theory, say ZFC set theory. It might not be a straightforward question whether ZFC is logically consistent, but the question of whether a given theory is logically consistent is always a conceptual question regardless of whether the theory is a theory of set theory or physics or . . . .. So, if ZFC is logically consistent, it is a conceptual truth that ZFC is logically consistent. I assume that, in general, when it is a conceptual truth that if P, then Q, and it is a conceptual truth that P, then it is a conceptual truth that Q. So, given that it is a conceptual truth that ZFC is logically consistent, and that Conex is a conceptual truth, it is also a conceptual truth that there are entities that obey the axioms of ZFC.

Consider next a set theory S that seemingly competes with ZFC, but which is also logically consistent. There is an equally good argument for the conclusion that it is a conceptual truth that there are entities that obey the axioms of S. Might the entities that obey the axioms of ZFC be the same as those that obey S? To answer this question, we need to say a bit more about what it would be for two different set theories to compete. First, the two theories must be about the same relation, which in this case would be the putatively unique relation

---

[78] This idea is forcefully expressed in Hilbert (1980).
[79] This is the sort of view defended in Hamkins (2012).

denoted by the predicate "is a member of." Second, there must be entities such that the two theories imply logically inconsistent claims about how those entities are related by that relation. (There might be an overlap among these entities, but it is sufficient for one plurality of things to be collectively non-identical with another plurality when something is among one of the pluralities but not among the other.) On the set theoretic pluralism we are considering (on behalf of the proponent of easy ontology), one of these two claims must be false.

2.5 Restating the Hard Ontological Question?

Ontological realism – the claim that there are quantificational joints in reality – was introduced partly as bulwark against Hirsch's quantifier variantism.[80] The idea was that even if it turned out that the ontological questions asked in ordinary language are trivially answered, there is still an interesting and non-trivially answerable ontological question that can be asked in Ontologese, which is (allegedly) a possible language in which all expressions correspond to metaphysical joints, including quantificational expressions.[81] In response to Thomasson's easy ontological approach, Sider (2011: 195–197) makes two claims: first, Thomasson's project of easy ontology is possibly threatened if ontological realism is true, and second, it is a substantive question whether ontological realism is true, rather than easy an question in Thomasson's sense.

Here is a summary of Sider's rationale for the first claim. A conceptual truth is a truth that is both *definitional* and *true*. Whether an interpretation of a language is charitable is a function of whether that interpretation maximizes the truth value of sentences in that language that speakers of it are disposed to sincerely assert in appropriate conditions; but some sentences are such that it is more important to determining how charitable an interpretation is: A sentence is *definitional* when interpreting it as false makes an interpretation far less charitable than making other sentences false. However, the extent to which an interpretation is charitable is not the only factor that determines whether the interpretation is true: It also matters how natural the entities referred to by expressions give that interpretation. These scales can pull in different directions, and so it is in principle possible that the correct interpretation of a language is one which some definitional claims are nonetheless false. Sider suggests that conditionals like "If there are as many shoes are as there are feet, then the number of shoes is the same as the number of feet" are definitional. But in order for them to also be *conceptually true*, there can't be a quantificational joint such that (1) there is an interpretation of "there are" that assigns to "there

---

[80] See Sider (2009).
[81] See Sider (2011; 2014); also relevant is McDaniel (2017: sections 1.4 and 5.4).

are" that quantification joint, and on that interpretation, this conditional expresses something false, and (2) the naturalness of that interpretation is strong enough to trump charity, and so even though these conditionals (and others like it) are definitional, the correct interpretation of them is one in which they are false. If there is such a quantificational joint, then these conditionals are false despite their status as definitional; let us call a quantificational joint that meets these two conditions a "doom joint." Ontology is easy only if there is no doom joint.

It's tempting to think that these three claims stand or fall together: the claim that ontology is easy, the claim that it is not a hard question whether there is a doom joint, and the claim that there is no hard analogue in Ontologese of an easy ontological question. Ontology is easy if and only if ontological questions can be settled wholly by empirical enquiry and conceptual analysis; if ontology is easy, then there is no doom joint. So, if ontological questions can be settled wholly by empirical inquiry and conceptual analysis, then there is no doom joint. But what is the status of that conditional? It seems to be a conceptual truth. And what is the status of the antecedent? If it is true, it also seems to be a conceptual truth that it is true. So, if we assume that ontology is easy, it seems that it follows that it is a conceptual truth that there is no doom joint. Is it a conceptual truth that there is no doom joint? If there is a quantificational joint, it's hard to see how it could be a conceptual truth that there is no doom joint. However, it is a conceptual truth that if there are no quantificational joints at all, then there is no doom joint. So, if it is a conceptual truth that there are no quantificational joints at all, it is also a conceptual truth that there is no doom joint.

It seems then that the best way to defend the project of easy ontology is to argue against the possibility of quantificational joints on conceptual grounds rather via some more abstruse metaphysical rationalization. Unsurprisingly, then, this is what Thomasson (2015: 300–317) does. She argues that there are a variety of functions expressions can have, and that there isn't a good reason to think that the semantic function of a quantifier is to carve the world at a quantificational joint. Instead, she suggests that quantificational expressions are *formal* expressions, where part of what it is to be a formal expression is that the question of whether that expression carves at the joints does not arise. In this respect, formal expressions would be akin to punctuations such as parentheses; it doesn't even make sense to ask whether "{" and "}" carve closer to the joints than "[" and "]." Perhaps "syncategorematic" would have been a better word choice than "formal" here, since the former expression was primarily used to refer to a class of expressions that do not correspond to entities, unlike, for example, names and predicates, whereas the latter expression has been used in a multiplicity of ways.

That said, it is not clear to me whether Thomasson thinks that words like "something" are syncategorematic. And there is a good reason to think that they are not. The standard semantics for quantifiers is one in which they are assigned semantic values, specifically, higher-order properties or relations.[82] Just as the easy ontologist refrains from criticizing the ontological commitments of mathematics on philosophical grounds external to mathematical practice, she should refrain from criticizing the ontological commitments of semantics on philosophical grounds external to linguistic practice.[83] Given this, the assumption that the quantifiers correspond to higher-order properties or relations is dialectally safe. But it is properties and relations that, in general, appear on the naturalness scale. Given that "something" corresponds to a property or relation, how can it not be an initially open question – one that is *not* settled by our concepts – where on this scale it is? Given that "something" corresponds to a property or relation, how can it not be an initially open question whether there are other property or relations that are possible semantic values for expressions that a function like "something" does in other languages? And how can it not be an initially open question whether one of these possible semantic values is either a perfectly natural property or relation, or at least more natural than any of the relevant alternatives to it?

Thomasson claims that it is not part of the semantic function of a quantifier that it carves nature at its joints. This might be true. But even if it is not part of its semantic function to do this, it might nonetheless do it! It is not part of the function of a hammer that it makes a good paper weight, and yet a given hammer can make a good paper weight. I doubt that it is part of the semantic function of a predicate qua predicate that it carves nature at the joints, yet many of them nonetheless do. And those that do not carve nature at the joints are not defective in the sense that they fail to fulfill their semantic function. Predicates have many semantic functions. One of them is to complement a noun phrase in order to produce a complete declarative sentence that is capable of being true or false. A predicate that failed to do this might be defective *qua* predicate, just as a name that fails to refer to anything might be defective *qua* name. But predicates like "blue," "grue," "in New Jersey," and so on are not defective qua predicates even though what they correspond to are not very natural properties. It seems then that some predicates carve nature at the joints better than others, presumably by virtue of denoting properties that are more natural than others, even though it is

---

[82] See again Westerståhl (2011).
[83] As a historical note, Carnap's (1956) inner/outer distinction was developed primarily to make the semanticist's use of abstract entities immune to criticism external to their practice.

not part of the general semantic function of predicates to carve at the joints. Why isn't the same then true of quantifiers?

2.6 Further Potentially Hard Questions

Suppose Thomasson is correct, and that many ontological questions are easy. Does any hard metaphysical question in the ballpark of the easy ontological question remain? For example, suppose that both the ontology of numbers and of physical objects is easy. Still, mightn't we wonder if numbers are *grounded* in physical objects, or vice versa? And isn't that question a hard question?

Consider the following biconditional: Something is perforated if and only if there is a hole in it. This biconditional is as obviously true as the other biconditionals of this sort that we have discussed; if these others are conceptual truths, this one is as well. Conversely, if the others are not conceptual truths, neither is this one. Instead, what is a conceptual truth is this conditional: If there are holes, then something is perforated if and only if there is a hole in it.[84] Accordingly, the question of whether there are holes is as easily affirmatively answered as the question of whether there are numbers or composite objects. Suppose then that there are holes. But holes and the physical things that host them – for example, bagels and donuts – are not metaphysically on a par, even if there is an easy argument for both.[85] The presence of a hole is explained by the existence of a perforated object; the direction of explanation in this biconditional is clear.

Others, however, are not. Many philosophers think that wholes are grounded in their parts. But consider this: Human beings are bilaterally symmetric. Something is bilaterally symmetric if and only if it has a left side and a right side. This biconditional also feels like as much of a conceptual truth as any of the others. So, human beings have left and right sides. A similar argument suggests that human beings have top and bottom halves as well. Left sides and bottom halves are parts. Now, I can see the case for the claim that the particles that make me up are metaphysically prior to myself. It's less clear though that my left half is metaphysically prior to me; these kinds of parts are sometimes called "arbitrary undetached parts," and I think part of why this label is apt is that these parts are not as fundamental as the wholes they are parts of. Either way, though, I think there are no obvious or easy metaphysical truths about grounding: Whether my left half is prior to or posterior to (or equal in priority with) me requires serious and systematic thinking.

---

[84] Compare with McDaniel (2017: 153–154).
[85] On the view I prefer, this lack of parity consists in the fact that holes have less being than their hosts; see McDaniel (2017: chapter 5, especially section 5.6).

Is the project of easy ontology threatened by the existence of hard metaphysical questions about grounding?[86] If the epistemology and methodology of questions about grounding must be the same as the epistemology and methodology of questions about ontology, then questions about grounding would be "easy" if and only if questions about ontology were. And if the former questions were hard, the latter would be as well. But we don't know that the epistemology and methodology of these questions must be the same. So, although it would be interesting to learn that there are still hard metaphysical questions even given the easiness of ontology, the former fact would not clearly be threatening to the latter.[87]

There are similar questions about ontological categories. For example, Flocke and Ritchie (2022) persuasively argue that even if there are easy arguments for the existence of a certain kind of entity, there can still be a hard metaphysical question about what the nature and structure of things of that kind, including the question of what ontological category they belong, are. For example, they note that Thomasson offers an easy ontological argument for events. But there are different theories about events. On one theory, events are individuated by the causal relations they stand in. On another theory, events are structured entities that consist of objects, properties or relations, and times. It seems that both theories can't be true. So, it seems that there is a hard metaphysical question about the nature and structure of events.

Perhaps though, if ontology is easy, these theories about events are not actually in competition. Perhaps there are entities that are individuated by their causal relations, and there are other entities that correspond to structures of objects, properties or relations, and times. (Though recall the earlier discussion about whether there are times.) Neither the former nor the latter are definitively *the* events. Instead, our conception of what events are is compatible with either being events. Rather than a hard metaphysical question about what events really are, we face soft questions about which richer conception of events is most useful to employ for a given purpose. In other words, the question is not what events are, but which conception of events we ought to use.[88] For example, perhaps the conception of events as individuated causally is more useful in the context of scientific explanation, while the conception of events as consisting of objects, properties or relations, and times is more useful in the context of assigning values to consequences or blameworthiness to agents. Given easy ontology, pluralism about events seems as plausible as pluralism about sets.

---

[86] See, e.g., Schaffer (2009).
[87] See also Thomasson (2015: 325–327) for a brief discussion of grounding and easy ontology.
[88] Compare with Thomasson (2017). See also Flocke and Ritchie (2022: 90).

Maybe there are many ways to be a set. Maybe there are many ways to be an event. Are there also many ways to *be* period? That's the topic of the next section!

2.7 Ontological Pluralism

Ontological pluralism is the view that there is more than one way to be. The rough slogan that all versions of ontological pluralism assert is that in addition to different kinds of beings, there are also different modes of being. Different versions of ontological pluralism spell out this slogan more in different yet (hopefully) more precise ways.[89] Here I focus on a version of ontological pluralism that is also reasonably called "quantifier pluralism."[90] On this version of ontological pluralism, modes of being correspond to possible meanings for existential quantifiers. But we have a choice point here: Perhaps any possible meaning for an existential quantifier is a mode of being, or perhaps only those possible meanings that are sufficiently metaphysically natural (in the sense of "natural" invoked by Lewis and Sider) are modes of being.[91] In McDaniel (2017: 37), I opted for the latter, and here I will presuppose a version of ontological pluralism that is true if and only if there is more than one relatively fundamental meaning for an existential quantifier, where an existential quantifier meaning is relatively fundamental if and only if no other quantifier meaning is more fundamental than it. For the sake of brevity, in what follows I will use "ontological pluralism" to designate this version of ontological pluralism unless context demands that I note that it is one version of ontological pluralism out of many.

By my lights, there is no case for ontological pluralism that is independent of considerations in first-order metaphysics and ontology. Accordingly, I will not focus on the reasons for accepting or rejecting ontological pluralism here.[92] Instead, I will focus on how ontological pluralism interacts with the other metaontological theses discussed here. Ontological pluralism occupies an interesting position in the dialectical space in which the views discussed earlier have been placed. Thomasson's easy ontology is a form of ontological monism incompatible ontological pluralism; her rejection of quantificational joints rules out ontological pluralism just as much as ontological realism. Sider's

---

[89] I discuss a variety of versions of ontological pluralism in McDaniel (2017). Also relevant are Caplan (2011), Rettler (2020), Spencer (2012), and Turner (2010; 2012; 2014).
[90] See Simmons (2022) for a discussion of and critical response to quantifier pluralism.
[91] Although this question is primarily a question of bookkeeping, I am chagrined to admit that I continue to be unsure which is a better way of keeping the books.
[92] McDaniel (2017) is where I describe various theoretical considerations that favor different versions of ontological pluralism. Czerkawski (2023) offers a "master argument" for ontological pluralism that does not rely on the sorts of theoretical considerations I appealed to.

ontological realism is also incompatible with ontological pluralism – though Sider permits that there might be many possible meanings for the existential quantifier, only one of them is relatively fundamental. (And by Sider's lights, that relatively fundamental meaning is itself perfectly natural.)

This leaves Hirsch's ontological deflationism. In McDaniel (2017: 37), I claimed that on this understanding of ontological pluralism, Hirsch's ontological deflationalism is a version of ontological pluralism. The reasoning was straightforward, though perhaps simplistic as well. Ontological deflationalism implies that there is more than possible one meaning for the existential quantifier, and at least two of these meanings are such that they are metaphysically on a par and at least as natural as any other possible meanings for the existential quantifier. But so understood then ontological deflationalism implies there is more than one relatively fundamental quantifier meaning – and hence implies ontological pluralism.

I anticipated that some would find this upshot surprising, since ontological deflationalism is supposed to be a deflationary view – it's in the name after all – while ontological pluralism seems to be a paradigmatically inflationary view. For what it is worth, in personal conversation, it seems that few have been convinced. A recent paper by Arturo Javier-Castellanos (2019) offers a general diagnosis of where things (allegedly) have gone wrong. Let's examine this diagnosis.

The ontological realist, ontological deflationalist, and ontological pluralist are each happy to talk of an ideal language for doing metaphysics. Javier-Castellanos (2019: 278) says that "a language is metaphysically better … than another to the extent that it allows for a more metaphysically perspicuous description of reality … [and] a language is ideal … if there is no better language"; he also notes that a similar characterization can be given for expressions: Some expressions carve nature at the joints more than others, and a fundamental expression is one for which no expression is more natural than it. Javier-Castellanos (2019: 278–279) claims that I (along with Sider (2011: 8) and Turner (2010: 421)) claim that a language is ideal if and only if every primitive expression in that language is a fundamental expression; Javier-Castellanos calls this "the simple analysis," and argues that ontological deflationalism is a version of ontological pluralism only if the simple analysis is true.

Javier-Castellanos (2019: 283) asks us to consider three languages that differ only in their primitive quantifiers: a nihilist language, a universalist language, and a common sense language. Let us assume that what the quantifier variantist will grant each of these is an ideal language. There is also a language – a pluralist language – that contains all three quantifiers. Given the simple analysis, this pluralist language is also ideal. Accordingly, if this version of quantifier variantism is true, a corresponding version of ontological pluralism is also true. Javier-Castellanos notes that one can't simply revise the simple analysis to say that a language is ideal if and only if an expression is a primitive expression of that language if and only if it is perfectly natural – since doing so yields that none of the nihilist, universalist, or common sense languages are ideal, contrary to this version of quantifier variantism.

Javier-Castellanos (2019: section IV) suggests that we need to rethink the relation between the idealness of a language and the naturalness of its primitive expressions. The simple analysis is an atomistic account of ideality, one that explains it in terms of the naturalness of its (discrete) primitive expressions. Javier-Castellanos suggests instead that the ideality of a language is explanatorily primary; an expression is perfectly natural if and only if it is a primitive of some ideal language or other (p. 285).

Given this holistic account of perfect naturalness, Javier-Castellanos (2019: 286) proposes new accounts of ontological pluralism and quantifier variantism. Here's the basic idea, although I'll modify a few of the small details. A quantified language is a language that contains at least one primitive existential quantifier expression. Ontological pluralism is the view that every ideal language is a quantified language that has multiple primitive existential quantifiers in it. To return to the toy example used two paragraphs ago, our quantifier variantist denies this claim: The nihilist language, for example, is an ideal language even though it contains only one existential quantifier expression. So, on this clever reconceptualization of these views, quantifier variantism does not imply ontological pluralism, and some versions of quantifier variantism are inconsistent with ontological pluralism. Javier-Castellanos (2019: 288) notes that some versions of quantifier variantism are also versions of ontological pluralism, but this is a weaker claim than the claim that all versions of quantifier variantism are versions of ontological pluralism.

Before considering criticisms of this proposal, let's see how, given this holistic account, other interesting metaontological views could be reformulated. There seems to be a straightforward way to formulate ontological realism: Ontological realism is the view that every ideal language is a quantified language, and every ideal quantified language contains the same existential quantifier expression. Since the "easy ontology" metaontological view is supposed to be inconsistent with ontological realism, perhaps this metaontological view should be formulated so as to imply that not every ideal language is a quantified language; if there are no quantificational joints in reality, then the absence of an existential quantifier should not automatically make the language less than ideal. Finally, ontological nihilism could be formulated as the position that no quantified language is an ideal language.[93]

---

[93] See O'Leary-Hawthorne and Cortens (1995) and Turner (2011) for a formulation and tentative defense of ontological nihilism.

I don't have strong feelings about this, but I do wonder about whether the formulation of ontological pluralism is apt. Let's consider two alternative formulations: one weaker than Javier-Castellanos's, and one stronger. The weaker one first: Instead of formulating ontological pluralism as the view that every ideal language is a quantified language that has multiple primitive existential quantifiers in it, formulate it as the weaker view that some ideal language is a quantified language that has multiple primitive existential quantifiers in it. On this weaker formulation, quantifier variantism might still imply ontological pluralism, provided that whenever there are some ideal languages that contain distinct existential quantifier expressions, there is also an ideal language that contains at least two of those distinct existential quantifier expressions. I do not know whether this proviso is true, however.[94]

Now let's consider a stronger formulation of ontological pluralism: Every ideal language is a quantified language that has multiple primitive existential quantifiers in it, and it is the same primitive existential quantifiers in each ideal language. This stronger formulation of ontological pluralism is inconsistent with Javier-Castellanos's formulation of quantifier variantism, and plays up the "inflationary" metaphysical aspect of the view. In fact, this formulation of ontological pluralism runs parallel to the formulation of ontological realism I offered in a pleasing way: Both ontological pluralism and ontological realism agree that every ideal language is a quantified language and that the quantifier expressions in each ideal language are the same, but they disagree about the number of existential quantifier expressions in them. This is a neat result.

As I said, I don't have strong feelings about any of this, largely because I regard the task of properly classifying a view as belonging to a larger family of views to be not unimportant but certainly secondary to the task of figuring out which view is true. If there are relatively natural classes of views, then how to classify a view might be a substantive question; I'm not sure that there is, however.[95] That said, it can be a substantive and important question whether the presuppositions of a classificatory system are correct – and so let's turn to the question about whether holism about ideal languages is true.

Let me state at the outset that if the sole reason for preferring holism over atomism is that we can better classify metaontological views given holism than atomism, then we have at best a very weak reason for accepting holism. It would be better if, for example, holism solved a genuine puzzle. Javier-Castellanos argues that it does (2019: 291–292) – it provides a solution to the problem of redundant natural expressions not available to the atomist. Recall the puzzle:

---

[94] Compare with Javier-Castellanos (2019: 284).
[95] Both Spencer (2012) and Caplan (2011) are sympathetic with the idea that the class of views properly construed as versions of ontological pluralism is a somewhat disjunctive class.

We have many collections of expressions where it seems that at least one member of the collection is highly natural – perhaps perfectly natural – but where it also seems like there is massive metaphysical redundancy if each of them enjoys the same degree of naturalness. Some examples are the existential and the universal quantifier; the various mereological expressions such as parthood, proper parthood, overlap, and so on; after than and before than; the truth functional connectives; and so on. Let's focus on the latter, since that is what Javier-Castellanos focuses on. But as he notes, there is a schema for a variety of views that he could be developed.

So, consider two pairs of connectives: the first of which consists of disjunction and negation, and the second of which consists of conjunction and negation. Each pair is sufficient to define all of the other truth-functional connectives, so the triplet consisting of disjunction, negation, and conjunction contains a redundant connective. Should we thereby say that none of these is a natural expression? Javier-Castellanos (2019: 291–292) suggests that we allow that each of them is a natural expression, but soothe our intuitions against redundancy in the following way: There is an ideal language that contains the first pair, a different ideal language that contains the second pair, but no ideal language that contains the triplet. If there were a third ideal language of that sort, then there would be genuine metaphysical redundancy.

What can be said against holism? It seems that given holism, there is no deep explanation of why certain languages are not ideal – languages whose lack of ideality seems best explained by the omission of certain expressions. Suppose that among the fundamental expressions are normative expressions.[96] Suppose that the remaining fundamental expressions are logical (including quantificational) expressions and those that come from physics. A language that contained only the latter would be incomplete even though it would be sufficient to characterize physical reality fully. And the reason why such a language would not be ideal would be that it was incomplete – it is missing other perfectly natural expressions. Holism is ill-equipped to make sense of that idea, since holism implies that betterness of language is prior to naturalness of expressions. Relatedly, there are other ways in which languages can fail to be ideal: In addition to missing natural expressions, they can contain primitive yet nonnatural expressions. There is a hard question about which way of falling short is worse – but in both cases, it seems that the explanation for why a language is less than ideal is the presence or absence of expressions. This fact seems to be reflected in intuitive sorting judgments. For example, we know that any

---

[96] That some normative expressions are among the fundamental ones is defended in McDaniel (2017b).

language that has "grue" as a primitive predicate is not an ideal language; its presence suffices for their nonideality.

Summary Remarks

I hope that this Element has given its reader a good overview of some of the elements of metaontology. While I am on the subject of hope: I suspect that for some philosophers the turn away from ontology toward metaontology was driven by the hope that metaontological questions would prove to be more tractable. However, as I believe this Element makes clear, metaontological questions are just as difficult as first-order ontological questions. There is no easy philosophical inquiry.

What to do then? Well, philosophy, of course. Our first-order ontological inquiries might benefit by connecting them to the discussions in metaontology, and, given my capacious account of metaontology, there is no way to do "pure" metaontology without also engaging, at some point, in ontology – and epistemology, philosophy of language, and even ethics as well. And, with respect to both first-order and second-order inquires, it is helpful to avail oneself to as much of the panorama of possible positions, arguments, questions, and considerations that can bring in to view. This is partly why I think that the study of the history of philosophy is useful to contemporary philosophy, and accordingly why the first chunk of this Element was occupied with some historical case studies. But philosophy also makes progress, and so we cannot remain only with our history.

References

Aristotle, *Metaphysics*, many versions.

Balcerak-Jackson, Brendan. 2013. "Metaphysics, Verbal Disputes and the Limits of Charity," *Philosophy and Phenomenological Research* 86.2: 412–434.

Bennett, Karen. 2009. "Composition, Colocation, and Metaontology," in *Metametaphysics: New Essays on the Foundations of Ontology*, edited by David Chalmers, David Manley & Ryan Wasserman, Oxford University Press, pp. 38–76.

Brenner, Andrew. 2023. "Theoretical Virtues and the Methodological Analogy between Science and Metaphysics," *Synthese* 201.54: 1–19.

Brentano, Franz. 1995. *Psychology from an Empirical Standpoint*, 2nd ed., translated by Linda McAlister, Routledge.

Bricker, Phillip. 2006. "Absolute Actuality and the Plurality of Worlds," *Philosophical Perspectives* 20: 41–76.

Burgess, Alexis, Herman Cappelen, and David Plunkett (editors). 2021. *Conceptual Engineering and Conceptual Ethics*, Oxford University Press.

Cameron, Ross. 2010. "How to Have a Radically Minimal Ontology," *Philosophical Studies* 51: 249–264.

Caplan, Ben. 2011. "Ontological Superpluralism," *Philosophical Perspectives* 25.1: 79–114.

Carnap, Rudolf. 1956. "Empiricism, Semantics, and Ontology," in *Meaning and Necessity*, expanded edition, Chicago University Press, pp. 205–221.

Czerkawski, Maciej. 2022. "Does Aristotle's 'Being Is Not a Genus' Argument Entail Ontological Pluralism?," *Archiv für Geschichte der Philosophie* 104.4: 688–711.

Czerkawski, Maciej. 2023. "Why Being Fragments," *Synthese* 202.196: 1–18.

David Hume. 1978. *A Treatise of Human Nature*, 2nd ed., Oxford University Press.

Dorr, Cian. 2004. "Nonsymmetric Relations," *Oxford Studies in Metaphysics* 1: 155–192.

Eklund, Matti. 2021. "Variance Theses in Ontology and Metaethics," in *Conceptual Engineering and Conceptual Ethics*, edited by Alexis Burgess, Herman Cappelen, and David Plunkett, Oxford University Press.

Felka, Katharina. 2016. *Talking About Numbers: Easy Arguments for Mathematical Realism*, Klostermann.

Fine, Kit. 1994. "Essence and Modality," *Philosophical Perspectives* 8: 1–16.

Flocke, Vera. 2021. "Ontological Expressivism," in *The Language of Ontology*, edited by J. T. M. Miller, Oxford University Press.

Flocke, Vera and Katherine Ritchie. 2022. "No 'Easy' Answers to Ontological Category Questions," *Philosophical Perspectives* 36: 78–94.

Frege, Gottlob. 1980. *The Foundations of Arithmetic*, translated by J. L. Austin, Blackwell.

Frege, Gottlob. 1972. "Review of Dr. E. Husserl's Philosophy of Arithmetic," translated by E.W. Kluge, *Mind* 81.323: 321–337.

Hamkins, Joel. 2012. "The Set-theoretic Multiverse," *Review of Symbolic Logic* 5: 416–449.

Hilbert, David. 1980. "Letter from Hilbert to Frege (29.12.1899)," in *Gottlob Frege: Philosophical and Mathematical Correspondence 1980*, edited by G. Gabriel, H. Hermes, F. Kambartel et al., Blackwell.

Hirsch, Eli. 2002a. "Quantifier Variance and Realism," *Philosophical Issues* 12: 51–73.

Hirsch, Eli. 2002b. "Against Revisionary Ontology," *Philosophical Topics* 30: 103–127.

Hirsch, Eli. 2005. "Physical-Object Ontology, Verbal Disputes, and Common Sense," *Philosophy and Phenomenological Research* 70.1: 67–97.

Hirsch, Eli. 2011. *Quantifier Variance and Realism: Essays in Metaontology*, Oxford University Press.

Hofweber, Thomas. 2016. *Ontology and the Ambitions of Metaphysics*, Oxford University Press.

Husserl, Edmund. 1982. *Ideas Pertaining to a Pure Phenomenology and to a Phenomenological Philosophy: First book*, translated by F. Kersten, Kluwer.

Husserl, Edmund. 2005a. *Logical Investigations, volume I*, translated by J. N. Findlay, Routledge.

Husserl, Edmund. 2005b. *Logical Investigations, volume II*, translated by J. N. Findlay, Routledge.

Javier-Castellanos, Arturo. 2019. "Quantifier Variance, Ontological Pluralism, and Ideal Languages," *Philosophical Quarterly* 69.275: 277–293.

Jenkins, Katherine. 2020. "Ontic Injustice," *Journal of the American Philosophical Association* 6.2: 188–205.

Kant, Immanuel. 1999. *Critique of Pure Reason*, translated by Paul Guyer, and Allen W. Wood, Cambridge University Press.

Kriegel, Uriah. 2017. "Brentano on Judgment," in *the Routledge Handbook of Franz Brentano and the Brentano School*, edited by Uriah Kriegel, Routledge.

Kripke, Saul. 1981. *Naming and Necessity*, Wiley-Blackwell.

Lewis, David. 1983. "New Work for a Theory of Universals," *Australasian Journal of Philosophy* 61: 343–377.

Lewis, David. 1984. "Putnam's Paradox," *Australasian Journal of Philosophy* 62: 221–36.

Lewis, David. 1986. *On the Plurality of Worlds*, Blackwell.

Lewis, David. 1990. "Noneism or Allism?," *Mind* 99.383: 23–31.

Linsky, Bernard and Edward Zalta. 1996. "In Defense of the Contingently Nonconcrete," *Philosophical Studies* 84.2/3: 283–294.

Linsky, Bernard and Edward Zalta. 1994. "In Defense of the Simplest Quantified Modal Logic," *Philosophical Perspectives* 8: 431–458.

Lotze, Hermann. 1884. *Lotze's System of Philosophy Part I: Logic*, translated by Bernard Bosanquet, Clarendon Press.

Ludlow, Peter. 2004, "Presentism, Triviality, and the Varieties of Tensism," *Oxford Studies in Metaphysics* 1: 21–36.

Lycan, William. 1988. "Review of *On the Plurality of Worlds*," *Journal of Philosophy* 85.1: 42–47.

Mally, Ernst. 1912. *Gegenstandstheoretische Grundlagen der Logik und Logistik*, Barth Verlag.

McDaniel, Kris. 2009. "John M. E. McTaggart, " *The Stanford Encyclopedia of Philosophy* (Summer 2020 ed.), Edward N. Zalta (ed.), https://plato.stanford.edu/archives/sum2020/entries/mctaggart/.

McDaniel, Kris. 2017a. *The Fragmentation of Being*, Oxford University Press.

McDaniel, Kris. 2017b. "Normative Accounts of Fundamentality," *Philosophical Issues* 27.1: 167–183.

McDaniel, Kris. 2020. *This is Metaphysics*, Wiley-Blackwell.

McMichael, Alan and Ed Zalta. 1980. "An Alternative Theory of Nonexistent Objects," *Journal of Philosophical Logic* 9.3: 297–313.

McSweeney, Michaela. 2019. "Following Logical Realism Where It Leads," *Philosophical Studies* 176.1: 117–139.

McTaggart, J. M. E. 1927. *The Nature of Existence, Vol. II*, Cambridge University Press.

Meinong, Alexius. 1904/1960. "On the Theory of Objects," in *Realism and the Background of Phenomenology*, edited by Roderick Chisholm, The Free Press, pp. 76–117.

North, Jill. 2018. "A New Approach to the Relational-Substantival Debate," *Oxford Studies in Metaphysics* 11: 3–43.

Novotný, Daniel. 2013. *Ens Rationis: From Suárez to Caramuel*, Fordham University Press.

O'Leary-Hawthorne, John and Andrew Cortens. 1995. "Towards Ontological Nihilism," *Philosophical Studies* 79.2: 143–165.

Paul, L. A. 2012. "Metaphysics as Modeling: The Handmaiden's Tale," *Philosophical Studies* 160.1: 1–29.

Plebani, Matteo. 2018. "Fictionalism versus Deflationism: a New Look," *Philosophical Studies* 175.2: 301–316.

Priest, Graham. 2005. *Towards Non-Being: The Logic and Metaphysics of Intentionality*, Oxford University Press.

Pyke, Stephen. 2011. *Philosophers: volume II*, Oxford University Press.

Raab, Jonas. 2020. "The Unbearable Circularity of Easy Ontology," *Synthese* 199.1–2: 3527–3556.

Rettler, Bradley. 2020. "Ways of Thinking about Ways of Being," *Analysis* 80.4: 712–722.

Rosen, Gideon and Cian Dorr. 2002. "Composition as a Fiction," in *The Blackwell Guide to Metaphysics*, edited by Richard Gale, Blackwell, pp. 151–174.

Russell, Bertrand. 1967. "Letter to Frege," in *From Frege to Gödel*, edited by Jean van Heijenoort, Harvard University Press, pp. 124–125.

Schaffer, Jonathan. 2009. "The Deflationary Metaontology of Thomasson's *Ordinary Objects*," *Philosophical Books* 50.3: 142–157.

Sider, Ted. 2014. "Hirsch's Attack on Ontologese," *Noûs* 48.3: 565–572.

Sider, Theodore. 2009. "Ontological Realism," in *Metametaphysics: New Essays on the Foundations of Ontology*, edited by David Chalmers, David Manley & Ryan Wasserman, Oxford University Press, pp. 384–423.

Sider, Theodore. 2011. *Writing the Book of the World*, Oxford University Press.

Simmons, Byron. 2022. "Should an Ontological Pluralist be a Quantificational Pluralist?," *Journal of Philosophy* 119.6: 324–346.

Spencer, Joshua. 2012. "Ways of Being," *Philosophy Compass* 7.12: 910–918.

Strawson, P. F. 1964. *Individuals: An Essay in Descriptive Metaphysics*, Routledge.

Suarez, Francisco. 2005. *On Beings of Reason: Metaphysical Disputation LIV*, translated by John P. Doyle, Marquette University Press.

Thomasson, Amie. 1999. *Fiction and Metaphysics*, Cambridge University Press.

Thomasson, Amie. 2007. *Ordinary Objects*, Oxford University Press.

Thomasson, Amie. 2009. "The Easy Approach to Ontology," *Axiomathes* 19.1: 1–15.

Thomasson, Amie. 2015. *Ontology Made Easy*, Oxford University Press.

Thomasson, Amie. 2017. "Metaphysics and Conceptual Negotiation," *Philosophical Issues* 27.1: 364–382.

Thomasson, Amie. 2021a. "What Do Easy Inferences Get Us?," *Philosophy and Phenomenological Research* 102: 736–734.

Thomasson, Amie. 2021b. "Conceptual Engineering: When Do We Need It? How Can We Do It?," *Inquiry* November: 1–27.

Turner, Jason. 2010. "Ontological Pluralism," *Journal of Philosophy* 107.1: 5–34.

Turner, Jason. 2011. "Ontological Nihilism," *Oxford Studies in Metaphysics* 6: 3–54.

Turner, Jason. 2012. "Logic and Ontological Pluralism," *Journal of Philosophical Logic* 41.2: 419–448.

Turner, Jason. 2014. "Donald Baxter's Composition as Identity," in *Composition as Identity*, edited by Aaron J. Cotnoir and Donald M. Baxter, Oxford University Press, pp. 225–243.

Twardowski, Kazimierz. 1977. *On the Content and Object of Presentations*, translated by R. Grossmann, Nijhoff.

Van Inwagen, Peter. 1990. *Material Beings*, Cornell University Press.

Van Inwagen, Peter. 1998. "Meta-Ontology," *Erkenntnis* 48.2/3: 233–250.

Warren, Jared. 2015. "Quantifier Variance and the Collapse Argument," *The Philosophical Quarterly* 65.259: 241–253.

Westerståhl, Dag. 2011. "Generalized Quantifiers," in *Stanford Encyclopedia of Philosophy*, https://plato.stanford.edu/entries/generalized-quantifiers/.

Wildman, Nathan. 2016. "How (Not) to Be a Modalist about Essence," in *Reality Making*, edited by Mark Jago, Oxford University Press, 177–196.

Williams, Donald C. 1962. "Dispensing with Existence," *Journal of Philosophy* 59.23: 748–763.

Williamson, Timothy. 2013. *Modal Logic as Metaphysics*, Oxford University Press.

Yagisawa, Takashi. 2009. *Worlds and Individuals, Possible and Otherwise*, Oxford University Press.

Zalta, Edward. 2006. "Essence and Modality," *Mind* 115.459: 659–693.

Zalta, Edward. 1998. "Mally's Determinates and Husserl's Noemata," in *Ernst Mally: Versuch einer Neubewertung*, edited by Alexander Hieke, Sankt Augustin: Academia Verlag, pp. 9–28.

Zalta, Edward. 1995. "Two (Related) World Views," *Nous* 29.2: 189–211.

Zalta, Edward. 1992. "On Mally's Alleged Heresy: A Reply," *History and Philosophy of Logic* 13: 59–68.

Acknowledgments

I have benefited from numerous conversations on these issues over the years from many philosophers. Special thanks to Ross Cameron, Daniel Nolan, and Joshua Spencer for discussing earlier drafts of this Element with me. I also received excellent comments from the anonymous reviewers, and I am grateful for their attempts to make this Element better.

Section 1 is partly based on my lecture notes for a graduate seminar Sam Newlands and I co-taught titled *Being and Nonbeing: Then and Now*. Sam is an amazing teacher and a friend. He is not responsible for any errors in this section, existent or nonexistent.

Tuomas Tahko was an excellent editor, and way more patient with me than I had any right for him to be. I thank him for putting up with me during this process.

I also thank my wonderful family for putting up with me all these years. I love you all: Charlie, Leneah, Nina, Pig, Rubix Porter, and Safira.

Cambridge Elements

Metaphysics

Tuomas E. Tahko
University of Bristol

Tuomas E. Tahko is Professor of Metaphysics of Science at the University of Bristol, UK. Tahko specialises in contemporary analytic metaphysics, with an emphasis on methodological and epistemic issues: 'meta-metaphysics'. He also works at the interface of metaphysics and philosophy of science: 'metaphysics of science'. Tahko is the author of *Unity of Science* (Cambridge University Press, 2021, *Elements in Philosophy of Science*), *An Introduction to Metametaphysics* (Cambridge University Press, 2015), and editor of *Contemporary Aristotelian Metaphysics* (Cambridge University Press, 2012).

About the Series

This highly accessible series of Elements provides brief but comprehensive introductions to the most central topics in metaphysics. Many of the Elements also go into considerable depth, so the series will appeal to both students and academics. Some Elements bridge the gaps between metaphysics, philosophy of science, and epistemology.

Cambridge Elements

Metaphysics

Elements in the Series

Grounding, Fundamentality and Ultimate Explanations
Ricki Bliss

Metaphysics and the Sciences
Matteo Morganti

Teleology
Matthew Tugby

Modal Naturalism: Science and the Modal Facts
Amanda Bryant, Alastair Wilson

Metaphysics of Race
Kal H. Kalewold

Metaphysics of Causation
Max Kistler

The Metaphysics of Gender
E. Díaz León

Reduction, Emergence and the Metaphysics in Science
Carl Gillett

The Metaphysics of Color
Michael Watkins and Elay Shech

Social Ontology
Brian Epstein

Neo-Aristotelian Metaphysics
Phil Corkum

Metaontology
Kris McDaniel

A full series listing is available at: www.cambridge.org/EMPH

For EU product safety concerns, contact us at Calle de José Abascal, 56–1°,
28003 Madrid, Spain or eugpsr@cambridge.org.

www.ingramcontent.com/pod-product-compliance
Ingram Content Group UK Ltd.
Pitfield, Milton Keynes, MK11 3LW, UK
UKHW031425300625
460082UK00018B/259